CONSUMER GUIDE TO

UNDERSTANDING & PROTECTING YOUR CREDIT RIGHTS

A PRACTICAL RESOURCE FOR MAINTAINING GOOD CREDIT

DANIEL A. EDELMAN

Cover design by Tony Nuccio/ABA Design

Printed in the United States of America.

21 20 19 18 17 5 4 3 2 1

ISBN: 978-1-63425-357-4

e-ISBN: 978-1-63425-358-1

Library of Congress Cataloging-in-Publication Data

Names: Edelman, Daniel A., author.
Title: ABA consumer guide to understanding & protecting your credit rights A practical resource for maintaining good credit / Daniel Edelman.
Other titles: Borrower and credit rights | American Bar Association consumer guide to borrower and credit rights
Description: Chicago, Illinois : American Bar Association, 2017.
Identifiers: LCCN 2017019660 | ISBN 9781634253574
Subjects: LCSH: Consumer credit—Law and legislation—United States. |
Credit cards—Law and legislation—United States. | Debit cards—Law and
  legislation—United States. | Credit—Law and legislation—United States.

  | Debtor and creditor—United States. | Consumer protection—Law and
  legislation—United States.
Classification: LCC KF1040 .E34 2017 | DDC 346.7307/3—dc23 LC record available at
https://lccn.loc.gov/2017019660

Discounts are available for books ordered in bulk. Special consideration is given to state bars, CLE programs, and other bar-related organizations. Inquire at Book Publishing, ABA Publishing, American Bar Association, 321 N. Clark Street, Chicago, Illinois 60654-7598.

www.shopABA.org

Contents

Introduction   vii

Chapter 1. Your Rights When Borrowing Money   1

Chapter 2. Understanding the Terms and Total Cost of Credit   5

Applicability of the Truth in Lending Act   6
    Closed-End Credit   6
    Open-End Credit   7

Chapter 3. Shopping for Credit Cards   9

Chapter 4. Negotiating a Home Mortgage Loan   13

Chapter 5. Mortgage Servicing   17

Chapter 6. Negotiating a Car Loan   19

Chapter 7. Obtaining a Student Loan   23

Chapter 8. Credit Card Rights   27

Credit Billing   27
Unauthorized Use   28
Defective Goods and Other Claims and Defenses   29
Other Rights of Consumers in Credit Card Transactions   30
Arbitration Clauses   33
Disclosure of Terms of Cardholder Agreements and Free Credit Reports   33

Chapter 9. Prepaid Cards   35

Chapter 10. Debit Cards and Electronic Fund Transactions
39

Chapter 11. Student Loan Rights
43

Chapter 12. Other Types of Loans
45

Payday and Auto Title Loans   45
Overdraft Protection   45
It Is Your Right to Know Why You Are Turned Down for Credit or Had Your Rate Increased   46

Chapter 13. Your Rights as a Debtor
47

Verification of Debts   49
Third-Party Contacts   50
Communication with the Debtor   51
Special Rules Regulating Cell Phone Calls   52
Abuse and Harassment   53
False, Misleading, and Unfair Acts and Practices   53
Where Collection Lawsuits May Be Filed   54
Unsophisticated or Least Sophisticated Consumer Standard   54
Damages   55

Chapter 14. The Collection Industry: Debt Buyers versus Original Creditors
57

Chapter 15. What to Do If You Are a Defendant in a Collection Lawsuit
61

Chapter 16. Defenses to Collection Claims
63

Bogus Charges on Credit Card Accounts   63
Capacity of Parties to Credit Card Accounts   64
Statutes of Limitations   64
Promises to Answer for the Debt of Another   65
Liability of Parents and Spouses   65
Liability of Children for Parent's Debts   66
Nursing Home Debts   66
Other Health-Care Debts   67
Automobile Deficiencies   69
Defective Goods and Services   70

Chapter 17. Dealing with Collection Calls
71

What to Say and What Not to Say   71
How to End Harassing Telephone Calls   72

Negotiating a Payback Arrangement   73
When to Contact a Lawyer Regarding Debt Collection   73

Chapter 18. Credit and Spending: Avoiding Common Mistakes and Borrowing Responsibly   **75**

Chapter 19. Your Rights with Respect to Credit Reports   **81**

Credit Scores and How They Are Calculated   83
Credit History   83
Amounts Owed   84
What Credit Scores Do Not Consider   84
Effect of Credit Inquiries on Credit Score   85
Improving Your Credit Score   85
Paying Off Collection Accounts   86
Foreclosures and Foreclosure Alternatives   87
Cleaning Up Errors on Your Credit Report   87
What Types of Information on Your Credit Report May Be Challenged   88
Who Can Get My Credit Report?   92
Are Reports Prepared on Insurance and Job Applicants Different?   92
Tenant Screening   93
Employment Background Checks   93
List of Tenant and Employment Screening Agencies   94

Chapter 20. Improving Your Credit Score   **95**

Chapter 21. When to Hire a Lawyer to Deal with a Credit Report Problem   **99**

Chapter 22. The Scope and Nature of Identity-Theft Crime   **103**

Who Is the Biggest Threat to Stealing Your Identity?   103
Common and New Types of Identity Theft   104

Chapter 23. Safeguarding Your Information from Identity Theft   **109**

Where Is Your Information Kept, and How Can You Keep It Safe?   109
Keeping Your Information Safe   109
Being Safe Online and on the Telephone   110
Suspicious Transactions   111
Watch What You Put in the Trash   112
Use Discretion in Private Places   112
Monitor Your Bank and Credit Card Statements and Credit Reports   112

Chapter 24. What to Do If You Are a Victim of Identity Theft **115**

Recognizing That Your Identity Has Been Stolen 115
Repairing Damage to Your Credit Report—Reports You Must File 115
Closing Accounts 117
Removing Unauthorized Charges from Accounts 117
Other Steps That You May Need to Take 118
    Tax-Related Identity Theft 118
    Opening New Accounts 118

Epilogue **119**

Index **121**

Introduction

The vast majority of Americans obtain credit at some point in their lives. Over 75 percent of Americans have at least one credit card. Credit also includes home mortgages, car loans, and student loans.

This book tells you about your basic rights with respect to obtaining and protecting your credit. It describes your rights under federal law and under common types of state laws. Federal law gives you extensive rights with respect to credit transactions, and all states have at least some laws on the subject as well. It also alerts you to common pitfalls in obtaining and using credit. It provides information about credit disclosures; negotiating common types of credit transactions; rights with respect to credit cards, debit cards, and other common transactions; debt-collection rights; rights with respect to credit reports; and identity theft.

Your Rights When Borrowing Money

Federal law and many state laws give you basic rights in applying for credit. These include the following:

- You have the right to shop for the best loan available to you and compare the charges of different lenders.
- You have the right to be informed about the total cost of your loan, including the interest rate and other fees.
- You have the right to have a clear understanding of the terms and total cost of credit. Disclosures setting forth the key credit terms must be provided to you in a form you can keep before you are bound to a credit transaction.
- You have the right not to be discriminated against in connection with a credit transaction—either refused credit or charged more for credit—based on race, color, religion, national origin, gender, marital status, or age; because your income derives from any public assistance program; or because you have exercised in good faith your rights under any title of the federal Consumer Credit Protection Act. The Consumer Credit Protection Act includes the Truth in Lending Act, Consumer Leasing Act, Fair Credit Reporting Act, Equal Credit Opportunity Act, Fair Debt Collection Practices Act, and Credit Repair Organizations Act.
- You have the right to have your performance on credit obligations reported accurately by credit bureaus *if* it is reported at all. Contrary to popular belief, there is no legal requirement that creditors report to credit bureaus unless they promise you to do so in a contract.
- You have the right to be informed if the information in your credit file has been used against you, to either deny credit or insurance or increase the cost of credit or insurance. This is done by means of what is generally called an *adverse-action notice*.

- You have the right to know what is in your credit file and to receive a free credit report from each consumer-reporting agency (credit bureau) once per year.
- You have the right to ask for your credit score.
- You have the right to dispute incomplete, inaccurate, or obsolete information in your credit file.
- You have the right to have your credit file used only for specified "permissible purposes," such as to review or collect an account or to evaluate a request for credit. (Although the written permission of the subject of the report is a permissible purpose, it is—contrary to popular belief—not necessary to obtain written permission if another permissible purpose exists, such as a request for credit.)
- You have the right not to be subject to deceptive marketing, servicing, and collection tactics regarding credit.

Several important warnings about applying for credit are also appropriate at the outset. First, under no circumstances should a consumer pay money in advance for arranging a loan, other than a modest application fee and fees for credit reports or appraisals for a mortgage or business loan. We have seen consumers charged $1,000 and more for application fees and assistance in applying for credit. They generally get nothing for their money. Advance-fee schemes are generally illegal scams.

Never provide incorrect information on a credit application.

Second, under no circumstances should a consumer ever agree to provide false information or documents in connection with an application for credit. Doing so has serious criminal and civil consequences. It is generally a crime to submit false information to a financial institution. The resulting extension of credit may be nondischargeable in bankruptcy.

Oral promises from creditors are worth the paper they are written on.

Third, review carefully any loan or other credit documentation you receive and make sure that it accurately states the terms of the intended transaction and contains all promises made to you. We hear from many consumers who claim that a lender or car dealer promised them that their rate would be reduced after six months. If it isn't in the documents, it is not enforceable.

Review any credit application you fill out to make sure it is accurate and complete. If any blanks do not apply to you, do not leave them blank; instead, insert "N/A" or "not applicable."

Certain businesses, such as car dealers and mortgage brokers, have been known to insert or alter information on credit applications. If you have any reason to suspect the accuracy of the information supplied to a financial institution through a third party, ask the financial institution for a copy of the information submitted in your name and confirm the request in writing. If it turns out that the copy that the financial institution has is not identical to what you believe you submitted, notify the institution immediately, in writing, of the discrepancy.

Also, beware if you fill out a credit application in handwriting and are then asked to sign what is represented to be a typed version of the same application. Compare the documents carefully. We have seen multiple cases where the typed document is not the same as the handwritten one.

Finally, if false or misleading information is submitted on your behalf, it is usually because the truth would result in your not obtaining the credit applied for or because the transaction is predatory and not in your interest. Many lenders, such as banks, are required by law to comply with "safety and soundness" standards, including a requirement that they only extend credit that they expect you to be able to repay without default. These standards protect both the public, which insures banks against failure as a result of excessive loan losses, and you, the consumer. The submission of false information by dealers and brokers is an attempt to circumvent these standards.

In some cases, lenders that are not subject to such standards or their agents have consumers fill out false applications as a means of covering themselves against liability for predatory lending. If challenged, they can claim that you defrauded them by submitting false information to obtain credit you knew you did not qualify for. Furthermore, although many of the laws discussed in this volume provide for an award of attorney's fees to a consumer to encourage enforcement of legal rights, attorneys are unlikely to take cases where the client is subject to a counterclaim for fraud. In a practical sense, a false loan application thus amounts to a waiver of your legal rights.

In the following chapters, we will discuss these rights.

Understanding the Terms and Total Cost of Credit

The principal law relating to the disclosure of credit terms is the federal Truth in Lending Act (TILA) (15 U.S.C. §1601 et seq.). TILA requires disclosures of credit terms in consumer credit transactions. TILA was originally enacted by Congress in 1967 to effectively adopt a new "national loan vocabulary" that means the same in every contract in every state (*Mason v. General Finance Corporation of Virginia*, 542 F.2d 1226, 1233 (4th Cir. 1976)).

TILA was amended by the Home Ownership and Equity Protection Act of 1994 (HOEPA) (Pub. L. No. 103-325, Title I, Subtitle B, 108 Stat. 2190, adding 15 U.S.C. §§1602(aa) and 1639). HOEPA imposed certain substantive regulations on home mortgage transactions with high interest rates or fees.

Multiple amendments were made to TILA in 2008–2011, including the Mortgage Disclosure Improvement Act of 2008, the Helping Families Save Their Homes Act of 2009, the Credit Card Accountability Responsibility and Disclosure Act of 2009, and the Dodd–Frank Wall Street Reform and Consumer Protection Act (Dodd–Frank Act) (Mortgage Disclosure Improvement Act of 2008, Pub. L. No. 110-289, Div. B, Title V, 122 Stat. 2654, as amended by the Emergency Economic Stabilization Act of 2008, Pub. L. No. 110-343, Div. A, 122 Stat. 3765; Helping Families Save Their Homes Act of 2009, Pub. L. No. 111-22, 123 Stat. 1632; Credit Card Accountability Responsibility and Disclosure Act of 2009 (CARD Act), Pub. L. No. 111-24, 123 Stat. 1734; Dodd–Frank Wall Street Reform and Consumer Protection Act (Dodd–Frank Act), Pub. L. No. 111-203, 124 Stat. 1376 (2010)). These amendments imposed numerous additional substantive regulations and disclosure requirements, mainly on mortgage transactions and credit cards. Some of these regulations and requirements apply to the subsequent administration or "servicing" of the loan as well as to its origination.

Applicability of the Truth in Lending Act

TILA applies only to transactions entered into primarily for personal, family, or household use, as opposed to business use. Generally, this means that over 50 percent of the proceeds of the transaction must be for personal, family, or household use. Transactions for personal use in which the amount financed exceeds $50,000 are not covered unless a security interest is taken in real property or "personal property used or expected to be used as the principal dwelling of the consumer" (mobile homes, cooperative apartments, beneficial interest in an Illinois land trust, ground leases, houseboats) (15 U.S.C. §1603).

Basically, TILA and Regulation Z require disclosure of several key credit terms, computed in a precise manner and using precise terminology. TILA divides credit into open-end credit (exemplified by a credit card or home equity line of credit) and "credit other than open end," or closed-end credit, such as a conventional mortgage or auto loan.

Closed-End Credit

The key disclosures for closed-end credit transactions are as follows:

- The "amount financed," which is "the amount of credit provided to [the consumer] or on [the consumer's] behalf" (12 C.F.R. §1026.18(b)).
- The "finance charge," which is "the dollar amount the credit will cost [the consumer]" (12 C.F.R. §1026.18(d)). It includes "any charge payable directly or indirectly by the consumer and imposed directly or indirectly by the creditor as an incident to or a condition of the extension of credit" (12 C.F.R. §1026.4(a)).
- The "annual percentage rate" (APR), which is the finance charge expressed as an annual rate (12 C.F.R. §1026.18(e)).

Do not obtain credit based solely on the monthly payment.

Consumers should always shop for credit, comparing the APR. Consumers should not agree to credit terms based solely on a monthly payment.

Car dealers, in particular, try to "sell" consumers deals based solely on the monthly payment. This results in consumers agreeing to increasingly lengthy credit terms, during which the consumer is "under water"—the amount owed exceeds the value of the car. This makes it difficult to sell or trade in the car.

For example, making $300 payments on a $10,000 debt at 10% APR will result in paying it off in 39 to 40 months, during which you will have paid $1,764 in finance charges. Making $300 payments on a $10,000 debt at 20% APR will result in paying it off in 49 to 50 months, with a total of $4,718 in finance charges. Increasing the rate to 30% will increase the duration to 72 to 73 months and the total finance charges to $11,770. Just looking at the $300 monthly payment hides the difference between $1,764 and $11,770.

Under HOEPA and the Dodd–Frank Act, there are additional disclosure requirements and substantive regulations for mortgage loans that exceed certain interest rates. For example, the consumer is allowed an additional "cooling-off" period, and prepayment penalties are forbidden.

The 2008–2011 amendments also added a number of substantive protections for mortgage borrowers. One is a requirement that payments must be credited as of the date of receipt (15 U.S.C. §1639f, as added by Pub. L. No. 111-203, §1464(a)). Another is that payoff balances must be furnished by a creditor or servicer within seven business days of a written request by or on behalf of a borrower (15 U.S.C. §1639g, as added by Pub. L. No. 111-203, §1464(b)). There are also prohibitions against influencing appraisers to inflate property value, and there are restrictions on late fees and delinquency charges.

Open-End Credit

The key disclosures for open-end credit are the APR and fees. Fees are disclosed separately and do not affect the APR. Other disclosures include a "Minimum Payment Warning" and examples of the length of time required to repay the balance if only the minimum payment is made (15 U.S.C. §1637(b)(11)).

There are disclosure requirements (a) for applications and solicitations (15 U.S.C. §1637(c)), (b) that must be made prior to opening an account (15 U.S.C. §1637(a)), (c) for periodic billing statements (15 U.S.C. §1637(b)), and (d) prior to renewal of an account (15 U.S.C. §1637(d)). Additional disclosure requirements apply if the open-end plan is secured by the consumer's principal dwelling, such as in the case of a home equity line of credit (15 U.S.C. §1637(a)).

There are generally no limits on the rate of interest that can be charged on a credit card. Prior to about 1980, most states had "usury" laws that imposed maximum rates of interest that a borrower could be charged and imposed substantial penalties for noncompliance (such as forfeiture of all interest, the entire debt, or double the interest or excess interest). When interest rates skyrocketed as a result of inflation at the end of the 1970s, some states removed these restrictions for some or all types of loans, including credit cards. In addition, in 1978 the U.S. Supreme Court decided that federally chartered banks could charge customers located anywhere in the United States those rates permitted under the law of the state where the bank had its principal office (this is referred to as the "exportation" of interest rates) (*Marquette Nat. Bank of Minneapolis v. First of Omaha Service Corp.*, 439 U.S. 299 (1978)). Many banks that issued credit cards promptly obtained federal charters and relocated their principal offices

TIP

Review any credit agreement before you agree to it, making sure that you understand all of its aspects. Consumers need to read contracts before they sign them. The law charges you with knowledge of the agreement whether or not you read it. Assume that oral representations about the contents of a document that are inconsistent with the actual contents are not enforceable; with a few exceptions, that is the general rule.

to states where the legislatures could be persuaded to eliminate restrictions on interest rates, notably Delaware, South Dakota, and Utah. This effectively defeated efforts by other states to regulate interest rates on credit cards, as they could neither impose such restrictions on federally chartered banks nor prohibit federally chartered banks from doing business with their residents.

Summary

The law requires disclosure of key credit terms. It is important that you obtain the disclosures, review them, and understand what you are getting into.

Shopping for Credit Cards

Credit card rates vary widely, from under 10 percent to up to 30 percent or more. Annual fees also vary widely. Compare the annual percentage rates (APRs) and annual fees (which are not included in the APRs for credit cards). Only approximately one-third of credit card users shopped around for their last cards.

In deciding what terms are important, first decide how you plan to use the card. If you intend to use the card as the equivalent of cash and pay it off every month, the APR would appear to be less important. However, the fact is that about 60 percent of Americans who have credit cards carry a balance, and many people who don't plan on carrying a balance do so because they encounter unexpected major expenses. Consider how you have actually used credit cards in the past. Unless you have not carried a balance for years and are immune from loss of employment, major expenses, or other circumstances that might result in your carrying a balance, you need to get the lowest-APR card that otherwise satisfies your needs.

Cards with the lowest APRs typically do not offer airline miles and other rewards.

If you have consistently paid off your balance every month and reasonably expect that you will continue to do so, then you may want to focus more on fees and rewards. Compare the value of the rewards you expect to receive (and use) each year with the annual fee you might pay. You should only look for rewards cards if you have above-average credit and you pay your bill in full each month.

Be careful of credit card advertisements. Some ads, particularly for subprime cards, offer a credit limit "up to" a certain amount if you qualify for the maximum. A low credit limit can be very detrimental. Because your utilization of credit is a major factor in determining your credit score, maxing out a card with a low credit limit can hurt your credit score. In addition, subprime cards are often "fee-harvester" cards, in which a major portion of the issuer's income consists of over-the-limit and other fees. The extent

Avoid misleading credit card advertisements.

to which such fees could be imposed was restricted by the Credit Card Accountability Responsibility and Disclosure (CARD) Act and the Dodd–Frank Act, but there are still some bad deals out there.

Many ads list multiple rates or a range of rates, and you won't be informed of the actual rate you will get until after you're approved. Don't assume you will get the lowest rate advertised. Would you be satisfied with the highest rate offered? If you are not comfortable with the rate you receive, don't hesitate to reject the offer and cancel.

If you intend to transfer your balance from one card to another, compare the interest rate you are paying now with the rate you'll pay over the life of the new card—not just the introductory rate. Also, most credit cards charge a fee to transfer your balance. So even though a 0 percent interest rate on balance transfers may sound appealing, it may be "too good to be true." A one-time fee of 2 to 5 percent of the balance you're transferring is common. Because 1 percent of $5,000 is $50, this is not insignificant.

Check for a penalty APR. The regular APR can increase drastically if just two payments are late—even one day late—within a six-month period. All credit card offers must tell you what the penalty rate is, what triggers it, and how long it will last. Many subprime credit card issuers plan on making a major portion of their income from penalty rates.

Check for different APRs for different types of transactions. If you intend to use the credit card for cash advances, the APR for cash advances may be much higher than that for purchases (1 to 7 percent higher). Also note how cash advances are defined. Certain types of transactions that you may not think of as a cash advance are treated as such. For example, Bank of America treats the purchase of foreign currency, money orders, or traveler's checks as a cash advance, as well as person-to-person money transfers, bets, and the purchase of lottery tickets, casino gaming chips, or bail bonds.

There is no grace period for a cash advance—cash advances begin accruing interest immediately.

Check what the grace period is. Many credit card issuers have reduced the minimum interest-free grace period from the traditional twenty-five days to twenty. The shortened grace period, in effect, decreases the time you have to get your payment in before interest is charged and increases your chances of being late on a payment. A few issuers have no grace period at all.

Check for fees. Again, fees are generally not counted in the APRs for credit cards. Common fees include an annual fee, a cash-advance fee, and a late-payment fee. If you'll be transferring a balance, take a close look at balance-transfer fees. Many subprime cards have unusual fees.

People often overpay for open-end credit. Be wary of retailers that offer 10 or 15 percent off a purchase if you open a department store card. Most store cards have higher APRs than you can obtain elsewhere. If you don't pay off the balance in full when you get the bill, the interest on the purchase for a couple of months can exceed any savings from the initial discount. Most such offers are not worth it.

CAUTION

Beware of store credit card promotions.

Make certain you are informed of the APR, fees, and material terms on any credit card issued to you. In 2013, the Consumer Financial Protection Bureau obtained a consent order against General Electric CareCredit for allowing medical and dental offices to arrange credit card financing for expensive procedures without making the required disclosures to the patients (*In re GE Capital Retail Bank*, 2013-CFPB-0009, available at http://files.consumerfinance.gov/f/201312_ cfpb_consent-order_ge-carecredit.pdf). We see repeated complaints concerning promotional credit offers by retailers in which consumers are promised that there will be no interest if the credit is paid off within a certain period. Consumers often do not understand when the period ends, whether payments will be required during that period, or what rate will apply if they do not pay off the credit by the specified date.

CAUTION

Beware of misleading promotional rates on credit cards.

Credit card interest rates are often negotiable. Banks compete for the business of persons who are likely to repay them. Many people receive mail from either their current banks or banks they do not presently do business with offering low- or zero-interest credit for various periods. Many of these offers specifically seek to have people transfer balances from other cards. However, there is usually a fee for transferring balances, so call your current bank or credit union first—if you have decent credit, your current bank may be willing to negotiate a lower rate, match a promotional rate, or waive annual fees to keep your business. Your bank won't lower your APR just because you've been taking care of your credit; you need to call the bank and ask.

TIP

If you are happy with your service but think you're paying too much in interest and fees, see if your credit card issuer will match or beat the terms and rate on the new card you're considering.

If you move your account and plan on closing your old account, do not close your old account right away. Continue to make at least the minimum payment until you know the balance transfer has been approved and executed and the balance on the old card is zero. There are a couple of reasons for this. First, balance-transfer offers often provide that the bank has the right not to honor the request. Second, if you have been carrying a balance at a rate greater than zero, the standard methods of computing interest on credit cards will result in "trailing interest." What this means is that if you receive a statement showing a balance of $1,000 and have carried a balance during the preceding period, paying $1,000 by the due date on the statement will *not* result in paying off the account. If you mail a check for $1,000 by the due date, you will receive a statement the following month for interest on the $1,000. Furthermore, this will occur every month until the "trailing interest" is a trivial amount. You can call the bank and get the amount that, if received by a certain date, will result in the account being paid off, or you can estimate the interest and send it along with the $1,000.

Therefore, wait until you have confirmed a zero balance before you close the old account.

If you are applying for a home mortgage, wait until you have closed on the loan before applying for a new credit card. Although new credit card applications do not have a major impact on credit scores, mortgage lenders do not like to see applicants requesting new lines of credit before they close on a loan.

Be careful with cards offering "no preset spending limit." This does not mean that there is no credit limit. What it means is that a card's spending limit is determined on a month-to-month basis and that the issuer will not inform you (or the credit bureaus) of what it is at any time. This creates the possibility that your card will be unexpectedly declined. In addition, with such a card, the amount of credit used is compared to the high balance. This may adversely affect your credit score.

Summary

Select a credit card based on how you have actually used credit cards in the past. Look for rewards cards only if you have above-average credit and pay in full each month. Beware of promotions. Consider asking for better terms from your existing credit card company.

Negotiating a Home Mortgage Loan

If you are looking for a home mortgage, the most important advice is to shop around for the best rate. Compare the annual percentage rates (APRs) offered by various lenders and brokers. This may be the largest and most important loan you get during your lifetime.

The law entitles you to a good-faith estimate setting forth all loan and settlement charges before you agree to the loan and pay any fees (Real Estate Settlement Procedures Act, 12 U.S.C. §2601 et seq.). You have the right to know what fees are not refundable if you decide to cancel or not proceed with the loan agreement.

Check if you are eligible for a loan insured through the Federal Housing Administration (FHA) or guaranteed by the Department of Veterans Affairs or similar programs operated by cities or states. These programs usually require a smaller down payment. Under FHA programs, for example, persons with a Fair Isaac Corporation (FICO) score above 580 may qualify for a 3.5 percent down payment. Borrowers with lower scores may have to put down at least 10 percent. There is an upfront charge of 2.25 percent for mortgage insurance.

Mortgage loans can have a fixed-interest rate or a variable-interest rate. Fixed-rate loans have the same principal and interest payments throughout the duration of the loan term. Variable-rate loans, or adjustable-rate mortgages, can have any one of a number of "indexes" and "margins" that will determine how and when the rate and payment amount change. The length of the loan can be up to forty years. Loans may have equal monthly payments, changing payments, or a large "balloon" payments after a certain number of years.

The price of a home mortgage loan is often stated in terms of an interest rate, points, and other fees. A "point" is a fee that equals 1 percent of the loan amount. Often, you can pay fewer points in exchange for a higher interest rate or more points for a lower rate.

Find out if your loan will have a charge or a fee for paying all or part of the loan before payment is due ("prepayment penalty").

Fees and charges that you may have to pay upon application include application fees, appraisal fees, loan-processing fees, and credit report fees. Fees that you may have to pay before closing include those for a new survey, mortgage insurance, and title insurance. Also ask about fees for document preparation, underwriting, and flood certification.

Mortgage insurance is insurance protecting the lender against your default. Lenders often require mortgage insurance for loans where the down payment is less than 20 percent of the sales price. Mortgage insurance may be billed monthly, annually, by an initial lump sum, or through some combination of these practices. Mortgage insurance is not credit insurance, which pays off a mortgage in the event of the borrower's death or disability. Although you are charged for mortgage insurance, you derive no benefit from it other than being able to get the loan. If you should default on the loan and the mortgage insurance company has to make good on the insurance, it generally has the right to sue you for the amount it paid.

Find out if mortgage insurance is required and how much it will cost. It may be possible to cancel mortgage insurance at some point, such as when your loan balance is reduced to a certain amount.

You may also be offered "lender-paid" mortgage insurance (LPMI). Under LPMI plans, the lender purchases the mortgage insurance and pays the premiums to the insurer. The lender will increase your interest rate to pay for the premiums.

TIP

"Locking in" your rate or points at the time of application or during the processing of your loan will keep the rate and/or points from changing until settlement or closing of the escrow process. Ask if there is a fee to lock in the rate and whether the fee reduces the amount you have to pay for points. Find out the length of the lock-in period, what happens if it expires, and whether the lock-in fee is refundable if your application is rejected.

In addition to principal and interest, part of your monthly payment may be deposited into an escrow account (also known as a reserve or impound account) so that your lender or servicer can pay your real estate taxes, property insurance, mortgage insurance, and/or flood insurance. Ask if you will be required to set up an escrow or impound account for taxes and insurance payments.

Most lenders will not lend you money to buy a home in a flood-hazard area unless you pay for flood insurance. Some government loan programs will not allow you to purchase a home that is located in a flood-hazard area. Your lender may charge you a fee to check for flood hazards. You should be notified if flood insurance is required.

Many mortgage loans are arranged by brokers. Brokers offer to find you a mortgage lender willing to make you a loan. Some brokers act as your representative; some operate as an independent business and may not be acting in your interest. Your mortgage broker may be paid by the lender, by you as the borrower, or both.

You have the right to ask your mortgage broker to explain exactly what it will do for you—including whether the broker is representing you—and to have that set forth in a written agreement. You also have the right to know how much the mortgage broker is getting paid by you and the lender for your loan.

The website of the Department of Housing and Urban Development offers the resource "Shopping for Your Home Loan," which addresses the entire process of purchasing real estate (http://portal.hud.gov/hudportal/documents/huddoc?id=DOC_12893.pdf).

A 2013 study by the Consumer Financial Protection Bureau found that about half of mortgage borrowers don't shop for credit (https://www.consumerfinance.gov/about-us/blog/nearly-half-of-mortgage-borrowers-dont-shop-around-when-they-buy-a-home/). Most borrowers consider only a single lender or broker before deciding where to apply, apply with only a single lender or broker (77 percent), and rely on information from people with something to sell (70 percent), who cannot be relied upon to provide unbiased information. A significant number consider it important to have an established relationship with the lender, which substantially reduces the likelihood that they will look elsewhere for a better deal. Needless to say, such behavior is likely to result in consumers paying more than necessary. Although many of the riskier features are no longer permitted or available, there are significant differences among mortgage loans and terms.

The Truth in Lending Act (TILA) gives a homeowner rescission rights when the principal residence is used to secure an extension of credit for a purpose other than for the initial purchase or construction of the residence (15 U.S.C. §1635; 12 C.F.R. §1026.23). A creditor must furnish two properly filled-out copies of a notice of the right to cancel to everyone whose ownership interest in the principal residence is subject to the creditor's security interest. This is not limited to the borrower; for example, a resident spouse or child who is listed on the title has the right to cancel and must be notified of that right. The rescission right is not limited to real property but also includes mobile homes and interests in cooperative apartments. A residence held in a land trust is also covered if the other requirements (personal purpose, etc.) are satisfied.

The right to cancel normally extends for three business days using a peculiar definition of business day (i.e., excluding federal holidays and Sundays, but not Saturdays) (15 U.S.C. §1635(a)). However, if a creditor fails to furnish the "material disclosures" (listed at 12 C.F.R. §1026.23 n.48) and two properly filled-out notices of the right to cancel to each person entitled thereto, the right continues until (a) the creditor cures the violation by providing new disclosures and a new cancellation

WARNING

The right to cancel is not, and should not be considered as, a substitute for shopping for credit prior to signing a deal when you are not under time pressure.

period and conforming the loan terms to the disclosures, (b) the property is sold, or (c) three years expire (12 C.F.R. §1026.23(a)(3)). The right may be asserted against any assignee of the loan (15 U.S.C. §1641(c)).

Summary

Shop around for the best rate on a home mortgage. This is the most important credit transaction most people engage in, and it should be entered into with care.

Mortgage Servicing

A mortgage "servicer" is the company to which the borrower is instructed to make periodic payments. It is quite common to both sell mortgage loans and sell the right to collect or "service" loans. The consumer is entitled to written notice of both a transfer of ownership of a mortgage loan (15 U.S.C. §1641(g)) and a transfer of servicing of a mortgage loan (Real Estate Settlement Procedures Act, 12 U.S.C. §2605).

Mortgage servicers frequently commit errors in servicing loans. Some of these are accidental, whereas some are not.

Borrowers do not have the right to select who will service their loans. Mortgage servicers compete for the business of mortgage owners. They compete by offering to service the loans for a fee; the servicer offering to service for the smallest fee gets the business. In addition, the servicers get to keep the "servicing income" generated by the loans. The servicing income includes late fees, fees generated by the "forced placement" of hazard insurance, property inspection fees, and similar fees. Mortgage companies therefore have an incentive to increase the servicing income—the fees charged to the borrowers—in order to reduce the amounts paid by the mortgage owners. This situation—called reverse competition by economists—is very bad for borrowers because it gives the mortgage servicer an incentive to impose unauthorized, improper, or inflated charges.

To curb some of the abuses, the law gives certain rights to borrowers.

A borrower has the right to submit a "qualified written request" or "notice of error" to a mortgage company (12 U.S.C. §2605). You must send such a notice or request to the address specified for that purpose on the monthly statement, not to the place where payments are sent or to a general correspondence address. Include your name, address, Social Security number, and loan number. State in as much detail as possible what you think the mortgage company has done

Submit a qualified written request or notice of error to a mortgage servicer every time you get a statement or document that you do not agree with or fully understand.

wrong; however, do not delay sending a request or notice while you collect documentation supporting your position. It is generally helpful to request an account history from the inception of the loan if the problem concerns fees, charges, or the crediting of payments.

The mortgage company has five days to acknowledge the request and must respond substantively within thirty days, either correcting the error and explaining why or stating reasons why it disagrees that there is an error. There are statutory damages for noncompliance.

In addition, the mortgage servicer may not take any adverse action with respect to the subject of a request or notice, including adverse credit reporting, until it responds substantively. For this reason, if you receive a series of statements or notices repeating the same error—for example, a balance that does not credit a payment that you have made, send a request/notice in response to each.

This right may be exercised with respect to a past servicer—where one company has transferred servicing to another or where a loan is paid off—for one year after the transfer of servicing.

Servicers need not respond if a request is duplicative, overbroad, or untimely or is not related to the borrower's mortgage loan account.

Certain Internet sites offer very long and detailed request forms, usually dealing with loan origination and disclosures rather than servicing issues. We advise against submitting such requests. Courts regard them as harassing and illegitimate, and lawsuits based on such requests get a very negative reception. If you have a specific issue, address it, explaining what the problem is.

Do not use elaborate qualified written request forms obtained on the Internet.

Summary

You have the right to challenge in writing anything done by or received from a mortgage servicer that you disagree with. You should exercise that right promptly and consistently.

CHAPTER 6

Negotiating a Car Loan

Consumers interested in financing a car should inquire as to available rates on their own from at least one lender and not just trust or rely on the car dealer. This is because the dealer may not give you the best rate. Dealers are legally allowed to "mark up" the rate offered to the consumer and keep part of the finance charges.

There have been persistent complaints that dealer mark-ups are influenced by the race, ethnicity, and gender of the consumer. In December 2013, Ally Financial Inc. and Ally Bank (the new name of General Motors Acceptance Corporation) settled a fair-lending complaint filed by the Consumer Financial Protection Bureau (CFPB) and the Department of Justice (DOJ) (CFPB No. 2013-CFPB-0010; *United States v. Ally Financial, Inc.*, 13cv15180 (E.D.Mich., Dec. 23, 2014)). The CFPB and DOJ alleged that Ally published a "buy rate" to dealers that reflected the minimum interest rate at which Ally would purchase a retail installment sales contract, but Ally would permit dealers discretion to mark up the buy rate to a higher rate in the retail installment contracts they entered into with auto buyers. Although Ally limited the dealer markup to 2 to 2.5 percent, it did not monitor whether impermissible discrimination occurred through the discretion that its lending policy and practice gave to dealers. The CFPB and DOJ estimated that over a period of thirty months, about 100,000 African American consumers were charged approximately 0.29 percent more in dealer markup than similarly situated white consumers, resulting in an average overpayment of $300 in interest over the life of the contract, and that about 125,000 Hispanic consumers were charged approximately 0.2 percent more in dealer markup than similarly situated white consumers, resulting in an average overpayment of over $200 in interest over the life of the contract. Ally agreed to pay $98 million in reimbursement and penalties.

In July 2015, American Honda Finance entered into a similar consent decree resolving similar allegations made by the CFPB and DOJ. According to the CFPB, Honda's past practices resulted in thousands of African American, Hispanic, Asian, and Pacific Islander borrowers paying higher interest rates than white borrowers for their auto loans, regardless of their creditworthiness. As part of the consent order, Honda agreed to change its pricing and compensation system to substantially reduce dealer discretion and minimize the risks of discrimination, and it was ordered to pay $24 million in restitution to affected borrowers (http://www.consumerfinance.gov/newsroom/cfpb-and-doj-reach-resolution-with-honda-to-address-discriminatory-auto-loan-pricing).

Subsequently, BMO Harris (Chicago, Illinois) and BB&T (Winston-Salem, North Carolina) announced that they would abandon dealer markups and pay a flat fee of 3 percent to dealers for originating contracts. Most auto dealers and other lenders have resisted abandoning discretionary markups.

Understand what annual percentage rate (APR) you are being offered, and compare the APR offered by the dealer with those offered by other lenders, including not only car dealers but also banks and credit unions (whose rates do not include discretionary auto-dealer markups).

If the rate offered by the dealer is competitive, there is one major advantage to having the dealer arrange financing. If there is a serious problem with the transaction, such as fraud, odometer rollbacks, a seriously nonfunctioning car, or the failure of the dealer to pay off a trade-in, in the case of dealer-arranged financing—*but not consumer-arranged financing*—the consumer is entitled to assert the problem as a defense to the payment obligation. The Federal Trade Commission requires the retail installment contract or other financing obligation to include the following statement: "NOTICE: ANY HOLDER OF THIS CONSUMER CREDIT CONTRACT IS SUBJECT TO ALL CLAIMS AND DEFENSES WHICH THE DEBTOR COULD ASSERT AGAINST THE SELLER OF GOODS OR SERVICES OBTAINED PURSUANT HERETO OR WITH THE PROCEEDS HEREOF. RECOVERY HEREUNDER BY THE DEBTOR SHALL NOT EXCEED AMOUNTS PAID BY THE DEBTOR HEREUNDER" (16 C.F.R. §433.2, "Preservation of consumers' claims and defenses, unfair or deceptive acts or practices").

The right to assert claims against the finance company is an important advantage in litigation by consumers against the dealer. The finance company generally has a contractual right to require the dealer to repurchase paper under such circumstances, which tends to force the dealer to agree to a reasonable resolution.

However, unlike the case with some mortgages, you generally do *not* have a right to cancel a car purchase or financing transaction within three days. The only cases in which such a right is granted by federal law are (1) where a mortgage on your home is taken as security for a car loan (should not happen) or (2) the car dealer's representatives visited you at home to obtain your signature without your visiting the dealer. Some used-car dealers may give a right to cancel a transaction within a specified period, but this is entirely a matter of contract. Make sure that any promise that you can cancel is in a signed writing.

Many people assume that such a right exists when it does not.

As noted in a previous chapter, car dealers often try to "sell" consumers deals based solely on the monthly

To facilitate comparison shopping, you are entitled to a copy of the truth-in-lending disclosures at the time you sign.

TIP

There is generally no right to cancel a vehicle purchase within three days or any other length of time.

WARNING

payment. This results in consumers agreeing to increasingly lengthy credit terms. If the APR is high, the term of the credit may be extended out six or seven years, during which the consumer is "under water"—the amount owed exceeds the value of the car. In addition to abusive markups, negotiating based on the monthly payment also invites car dealers to "pack" the transaction with credit insurance, overpriced extended warranties, and similar products, claiming that they don't increase the monthly payment. What they increase is the length of the credit obligation and the amount of finance charges paid. If the consumer trades the car in before the credit is paid off, the outstanding obligation is generally rolled over into the next loan.

One of the products dealers include in the transaction is "gap" protection. This is an agreement that if the car is totaled (destroyed or stolen) and insured, the consumer will not be held liable for the difference between the amount the insurance company pays and the credit obligation. See if your auto insurer will provide such coverage—if it does, it is cheaper than getting it from the dealer.

Look carefully at the payment schedule. See if there is a large "balloon" payment. If there is, make sure that you are able to pay it or have the right to refinance it.

Servicing of car loans presents some of the same problems as servicing of mortgages. For example, in May 2014, Consumer Portfolio Services, Inc., a major servicer of auto loans, entered into a consent order with the Federal Trade Commission, which alleged that it had collected money that consumers did not owe from over 120,000 persons. The consent order also permanently enjoined the lender from assessing or collecting any amount that is not (1) authorized and clearly disclosed by the loan agreement and not prohibited by law, (2) expressly permitted by law and not prohibited by the loan agreement, or (3) a reasonable fee for a specific service requested by a consumer after such fee is clearly disclosed and explicit consent is obtained. The lender was also prohibited from modifying the terms and conditions of a consumer's loan agreement through a loan extension or otherwise without the consumer's written "express informed consent" (*United States v. Consumer Portfolio Services, Inc.*, 14cv819 (C.D.Cal., June 11, 2014)).

A recurrent problem with auto financing is the failure of car dealers to pay off the loan balance on trade-in vehicles. Some states require a payoff within a specified time after the dealer obtains possession; for example, Illinois requires twenty-one calendar days (Illinois 815 ILCS 505/2ZZ). Regardless, the failure of a dealer to comply is a problem for the consumer. If the dealer pays late, the late payments will show up on the consumer's credit report. If the dealer fails to pay and the consumer arranged his or her own financing, the consumer may have no recourse. If the dealer fails to pay and the dealer arranged financing, the consumer may be entitled to recover from the finance company but probably has a lawsuit on his or her hands.

If at all possible, consumers should pay the existing loan off themselves prior to trading in the vehicle securing the loan.

If you can, pay off the loan on a trade-in vehicle yourself.

Summary

Shop around for auto credit. Because car dealers often mark up the rate, get a quote from a bank or credit union. Do not choose on the basis of the monthly payment.

Obtaining a Student Loan

In 2010, two-thirds of graduates from four-year colleges obtained educational loans. Consider carefully the debt burden that will result from financing an education, the likelihood that you will be able to find a job using the education, and the likelihood that the education will allow you to pay the debt burden. There are recurring abuses involving private vocational schools that provide degrees and certificates that are of little or no use in getting a job but are very expensive.

Before getting a loan, check for federal, state, and local grants and scholarships. There are numerous state and local programs as well as scholarships from educational institutions. Service members, veterans, and their families may be eligible for GI Bill benefits or military tuition assistance.

There are two basic types of student loans: federal student loans and private loans. For most borrowers, federal student loans are the best option. Some states offer subsidized state-sponsored alternative loans.

Federal loans are made or guaranteed by the U.S. Department of Education and have fixed interest rates. Recent rates have ranged from 3.86 to 6.41 percent, depending on the program. New rates were announced in June 2015, effective July 1, 2015; these are 5.84 percent on unsubsidized Stafford loans and 6.84 percent on PLUS loans. There is also a 4 percent loan fee ("points") on PLUS loans (made to the student's parents) and a 1 percent fee on other direct loans (formerly known as Stafford loans). The interest rate is lowered by .25 percent if you agree to automatic debits from your bank account.

Federal loans are generally cheaper than private loans, and it is generally easier to work out the repayment terms of federal loans. In the case of subsidized direct loans and Perkins loans, there is no interest while you are in school. Subsidized direct loans and Perkins loans require a showing of financial need.

Federal loans do have some downsides: there are draconian collection methods, including administrative wage garnishment and intercepts of tax refunds, and in most cases, there is no statute of limitations. A federal statute, 20 U.S.C. §1091a, eliminates the statute of limitations based on the type of loan and who holds it. Private student loans are generally subject to the statute of limitations. Governmental ones are not, if the loan is held by one of the entities referred to in 20 U.S.C. §1091a.

Also, you cannot borrow as much as from private lenders. Generally, undergraduates can get $5,500 to $12,000 per year, and graduate students can get $8,000 to $20,500 per year.

Other student loans are generally private student loans. The most common private student loans are offered by banks and credit unions. Their interest rates are often variable, which means your interest rates and payments could go up over time. Often, rates and payments can increase on short notice. Some schools and state agencies offer loans, which tend to have fixed rates.

Private loans can also be more expensive—rates have been as high as 16 percent over the past couple of years. There may also be origination fees or "points." In order to get a low rate, you may need to find a cosigner, generally a parent. In 2011, over 90 percent of private student loans required a cosigner.

There are some loan products that provide for the release of the cosigner after a number of timely payments. For example, Citibank provides for a release; Discover Financial Services does not.

However, 90 percent of consumers who apply for a cosigner release are rejected, according to the Consumer Financial Protection Bureau. Often, lenders require that a borrower make on-time payments for twelve consecutive months or longer in order to be granted a release. Even a day past the due date may disqualify you. There may also be qualifications relating to credit score, debt-to-income ratio, and length of employment. Lenders usually do not volunteer to release cosigners; it is necessary to know when you qualify for a release and actively apply for one.

Beware of promises to release cosigners on student loans.

Refinancing is an alternative. Some private student lenders offer refinancing.

NOTE: Both federal and private loans generally provide for a six-month grace period after graduation before repayment is required.

When it is time to repay, private loans don't offer as many options to reduce or postpone payments. On the other hand, private loans are sometimes subject to a statute of limitations, and they can only be collected in the same manner as other debts—the holder must sue you and obtain a judgment. Some private lenders or their debt collectors threaten to intercept tax refunds and Social Security payments, engage in administrative wage garnishment, or prevent you from receiving federal student aid in the future, but they cannot. Garnishment is permitted only where allowed by state law, and lenders have to obtain a judgment first.

At the present time, neither federal nor private student loans are generally dischargeable in bankruptcy. For recent loans, a court finding of hardship is required, which is difficult to obtain. (Old loans may be subject to more liberal standards, such as dischargeability after a number of years.)

For most people, federal student loans are a better deal than private student loans, so you'll want to take advantage of federal options first. To apply, fill out the Free Application for Federal Student Aid (FAFSA) and submit it early.

Summary

Exercise care in signing up for student loans. Consider whether the degree you are getting will allow you to pay off the loans incurred in obtaining it. If you can, finance your education with a federal loan rather than a private one. You generally cannot get out of a student loan through bankruptcy if things don't work out.

CHAPTER

8

Credit Card Rights

Credit Billing

The Truth in Lending Act (TILA) gives consumers the right to challenge billing errors and raise claims and defenses in credit card transactions.

Under the Fair Credit Billing provisions of TILA, within sixty days after receiving a statement of account first showing a charge, the consumer has the right to send a written notice to the creditor at the address given on the statement for disputes/inquiries (not the payment address) contesting the charge. The notice cannot be on a payment stub. It must give the account name and number, state that there has been an error in the bill and the amount of the error, and provide an explanation (15 U.S.C. §1666(a)).

Because of this limited period, it is absolutely essential that consumers review their credit card statements promptly upon receipt, check for any unauthorized or unidentifiable items, and complain about any such items in writing.

Billing errors include the following:

- that the item is not the consumer's;
- that the amount is wrong;
- that the consumer does not recognize the merchant name or transaction and wants documentary evidence of the charge;
- that goods or services were not accepted or not delivered in accordance with the agreement;
- failure to reflect payment/credit; and
- computational or accounting errors.

Billing errors do *not* include defects in accepted goods or services performed. The billing-error procedure also does not allow complaints about contract terms or disclosures. You may have other rights with respect to such problems, but they are not covered by the Fair Credit Billing provisions.

Some Internet sites and credit repair organizations advise consumers to send billing-error notices complaining about contract terms or disclosures. This is not sound advice.

Upon receipt of a billing-error notice, the creditor must

a. acknowledge receipt in writing within thirty days; and
b. within two billing cycles (and in no event later than ninety days) either
   1. correct the account; or
   2. conduct an investigation and send the customer a statement in writing explaining why the entry is correct and, upon request, send documentary evidence of obligation. (15 U.S.C. §1666(a))

The credit card issuer may not take any action to collect before conducting the investigation (15 U.S.C. §1666a(a)). If the account is reported to a credit reporting agency, disputed amounts must be shown as disputed (15 U.S.C. §1666a(b)).

Unauthorized Use

"Unauthorized use" is defined as use by a person other than the cardholder who does not have actual, implied, or apparent authority for such use and from which the cardholder receives no benefit (15 U.S.C. §1602(o)).

A person who is given a credit card by the account holder is an "authorized user" even if he or she uses it in a manner that exceeds the authority given by the principal cardholder. For example, if you give a card to the authorized user for the purpose of making one charge purchase in the amount of $100 and the recipient runs up $1,000 in charges, the charges are authorized because the merchant to whom the card is presented has no way of knowing of the restriction on authority. The only way to effectively revoke the authority is to have the account canceled.

Moreover, once charges appear on the monthly statement, if no objection is made, further charges of like nature may be "authorized." This could present a problem with estranged spouses and significant others. *If you do not trust an authorized user to make unlimited use of a card within the existing credit limit or any increased credit limit, cancel the account, and confirm any oral notice of cancellation in writing.*

Do not let other people use your credit cards—merchants and card issuers are not bound by any limitations you provide for the user.

Conversely, if the card issuer changes the address to which billing statements are sent without the consumer's permission, the consumer may not have liability.

It is not a good idea to allow others to use your credit cards or to have authorized users on your accounts.

We have seen schemes whereby cardholders are offered money to have strangers added to their cards as authorized users, for the purpose of building up the strangers' credit ratings. This is a very bad idea because you are liable for anything that the stranger does with the card. Also, credit card companies are taking steps to prevent this abuse.

A merchant who processes a charge for an excessive amount is not making unauthorized use of the card if the cardholder derives some benefit (e.g., if a car repair shop exceeds an estimate). However, there may be a billing error.

If the use was unauthorized, the maximum liability is $50 (15 U.S.C. §1643(a)(1)). That liability can be imposed only if (1) the card was an accepted credit card, (2) the card issuer has provided a method by which the user of the card can be identified as the person authorized to use it (such as a signature, photograph, or personal identification number [PIN]), (3) the card issuer has provided notice to the cardholder of potential liability and how to notify the issuer of theft or loss of the card, and (4) the unauthorized use took place before the cardholder notified the issuer that unauthorized used has occurred or may occur as the result of loss, theft, or otherwise.

If an issue arises as to whether a use of the card was authorized, the card issuer has the burden of proving the use was authorized within the rules described previously (15 U.S.C. §1643(b)). Again, however, furnishing a credit card to an authorized user makes essentially any use of the card "authorized" even if it contradicts the limitations given to the user.

Defective Goods and Other Claims and Defenses

If a credit card is used as a means of payment for goods or services (cash advances used to make purchases are not covered), a good-faith attempt is made to resolve the dispute with the merchant, the amount involved exceeds $50, and the transaction occurred within the same state as the cardholder's mailing address or within one hundred miles of that address, the credit card issuer is subject to claims and defenses arising from the purchase (15 U.S.C. §1666i(a)). The location of the transaction is normally the place of delivery for mail or phone orders.

The location and amount restrictions do not apply if the issuer and the merchant are the same or related entities (e.g., department store credit cards) or have a franchise relationship (e.g., gasoline company credit cards) or the merchant obtained the order through mail solicitation involving the card issuer (junk mail enclosed with the bill).

Creditors and assignees often argue that the failure to dispute a charge within two billing cycles pursuant to the billing-error procedures forecloses a consumer from later contesting the charge. This is wrong. The limitation of two billing cycles applies to your right to assert a billing error under the Fair Credit Billing provisions; it does not act to create liability. Furthermore, the claims and defenses that may be raised go beyond the billing errors cognizable under the billing-error procedure. For example, a breach of warranty with respect to accepted goods—the product purchased is defective and does not work properly—is cognizable as a defense but not a billing error.

WARNING

Failure to dispute a charge within two billing cycles does not make you liable for the charge.

Other Rights of Consumers in Credit Card Transactions

The Credit Card Accountability Responsibility and Disclosure (CARD) Act requires credit card companies to give consumers

a. forty-five days' advance written notice of a rate increase on a credit card before the increase takes effect;

b. forty-five days' advance written notice of "any significant change" in the terms of an open-end credit plan; and

c. a "clear and conspicuous" right to cancel upon any such change or rate increase (15 U.S.C. §1637(i)).

If the cardholder decides to close or cancel the account in response to such a notice, that decision may not constitute a default or trigger an obligation to immediately repay or to repay with less favorable terms or to be assessed any penalty or fee.

The CARD Act also limits a credit card company's ability to increase interest rates. A credit card company may increase credit card rates only

a. upon the expiration of a specified period of time not less than forty-five days and only with clear and conspicuous notice including a specified rate and not retroactively;

b. pursuant to a variable-rate agreement when the variable rate is tied to an index that is not under the control of a creditor;

c. at the end of and pursuant to a workout or temporary hardship plan and only with clear and conspicuous notice and in an amount not in excess of the rate charged in the same category of transactions charged before the plan began; or

d. after a minimum payment has not been made within sixty days after the due date and only with clear and conspicuous notice stating the reason for the increase and that the increase will terminate not later than six months after imposition if the creditor timely receives minimum payment. (15 U.S.C. §§1666i-1, 1666i)

These restrictions were aimed at abolishing formerly common "universal default" provisions, whereby one credit card issuer could increase interest rates because of a default on another card from a different issuer. This practice is no longer lawful.

If the consumer decides to cancel a credit card after a notice of a rate increase, the consumer may pay off any balance either in an amortization period of not less than five years or by making a required minimum payment of not more than twice the minimum payment required before the date of the increase.

The CARD Act requires the credit card company to review accounts every six months if the interest rate has been increased in order to determine if the factors that the company used to justify the increase are still in effect. If they are not, it must return to the old rate.

Payments made at local branches of a bank must be posted on the date the payment was made for purposes of calculating late fees (15 U.S.C. §1637(b)(12)).

Credit card issuers are now prohibited from charging an over-the-limit fee unless a consumer expressly requests the allowance of over-the-limit transactions (15 U.S.C. §1637(k)). The credit card company must provide advance notice of the over-the-limit fee. If the consumer elects to allow over-the-limit transactions, the credit card company must provide the consumer notice of the right to revoke the allowance each time the consumer incurs an over-the-limit fee. A credit card company may charge a consumer an over-the-limit fee only once during a billing period in which the credit limit is exceeded and only once during each of the two subsequent billing cycles unless (1) the consumer's credit limit is increased to exceed the amount by which he or she is over the credit limit or (2) the consumer reduces his or her balance below the credit limit by the close of the billing period.

Credit card companies are prohibited from charging consumers a fee for making a payment by mail, telephone, or electronic transfer. However, a fee may be imposed if the consumer utilizes an expedited service provided by a customer service representative and the cardholder agreement so provides (15 U.S.C. §1637(l)).

Penalties imposed by a credit card company must be "reasonable and proportional" to the violation of the cardholder agreement (15 U.S.C. §1665d). Certain charges presumptively comply with this requirement.

Finance charges may not be imposed for a late payment if the payment was received by 5:00 p.m. in the manner and location established by the credit card company.

Payment amounts in excess of the minimum payment must be applied to the balance with the highest interest rate, except in the preceding two billing cycles before a deferred-interest balance is due. For example, cash advances generally have a higher rate than regular purchases. Payments must be applied to the cash advances first. Similarly, if there is a zero-interest or low-interest promotional balance, these are paid off last. Previously, card issuers did the opposite—apply payments to the lowest-rate balances first.

Credit card companies are prohibited from charging consumers any late fees or finance charges for sixty days following the effective date of a material change in the credit card company's mailing address, office, or procedures for handling consumer payment that causes a material delay in the crediting of consumers' payments (15 U.S.C. §1666c).

The payment due date must be the same day each month. If the due date falls on a weekend or holiday, a credit card company cannot treat a payment received the following business day as a late payment (15 U.S.C. §1637(o)).

Credit card companies may not treat any payment as late unless the credit card company has adopted "reasonable procedures" to ensure that each billing statement is mailed or delivered to the consumer at least twenty-one days before the payment due date. If a credit card company provides for a grace period during which time a consumer may repay any portion of the balance

Credit card companies are prohibited from offering credit or increasing a credit limit without regard for a consumer's ability to repay (15 U.S.C. §1665e).

without incurring finance charges, the grace period must extend to twenty-one days after the periodic billing statement is mailed or delivered (15 U.S.C. §1666b).

Credit card companies may not use late payment or defaults on other debts as a basis for raising the rate on your credit card. "Universal default" clauses permitting such action were formerly common.

A credit card issuer may not increase the annual percentage rate (APR), fee, or finance charge within one year of the opening of the account or increase a promotional rate within six months of the date on which the promotional rate takes effect (15 U.S.C. §1666i2). Illusory "promotional" rates were previously a source of complaints.

The issuance of subprime "fee-harvester" credit cards is restricted. If a consumer is required to pay fees for the maintenance of a credit card account (other than late fees and over-the-limit fees) during the first year that the account is open, and the total fees exceed 25 percent of the total credit available, none of the fees may be charged to the credit card account (15 U.S.C. §1637(n)).

Special protections were created for minors and students. Credit card companies are prohibited from opening or issuing a credit card to anyone under the age of twenty-one unless the consumer has submitted a written application that (1) contains the signature of a cosigner who is over the age of twenty-one who has the means to repay debts incurred by the consumer and will be jointly liable, or (2) contains financial information showing that the consumer has an independent means of repaying any debt incurred. A credit card company must receive written consent from the cosigner before increasing the credit limit on a credit card account belonging to a consumer under twenty-one years of age. The cosigner will be jointly liable for the debt incurred as a result of the increased credit limit (15 U.S.C. §§1637(c)(8), 1637(p)).

There are additional protections for college students. Colleges and universities must disclose publicly any credit card marketing contracts between the institution and the credit card company (15 U.S.C. §1650(f)). Furthermore, credit card companies are prohibited from offering students at institutions of higher education any tangible item to induce the student to apply for or open a credit card account if the offer is made on the campus of an institution of higher education, near the campus of an institution of higher education, or at an event sponsored by or related to an institution of higher education.

These rules were designed to make it more difficult for people with bad credit and students to get credit cards.

Gift cards may not expire for at least five years, and inactivity fees generally cannot be assessed prior to twelve months.

Debit cards may pose greater theft risks than credit cards.

Debit cards linked to asset (checking, savings) accounts have a different set of rights, governed by the Electronic Fund Transfer Act.

Arbitration Clauses

Many credit and debit card agreements provide for arbitration of any disputes. This means that you give up your right to sue the credit card company. Disputes must be resolved by private arbitrators, whose proceedings are secret and essentially not subject to judicial review. Class actions are generally prohibited. We call arbitration clauses a "license to steal." Try to avoid them if you can.

Disclosure of Terms of Cardholder Agreements and Free Credit Reports

Credit card companies must establish and maintain an Internet site where they make cardholder agreements accessible (15 U.S.C. §1632(d)). They also must provide the Consumer Financial Protection Bureau with an electronic copy of each cardholder agreement, which it displays on a website. You can therefore determine if an agreement contains an arbitration clause or other undesirable terms.

Summary

You have the right to challenge billing errors in credit card transactions. You often have a defense against the credit card company if there is a problem with what you purchase. Be careful about who you allow to use your credit card. Unless you trust that person to make unlimited use of your card within the existing credit limit or any increased credit limit, do not allow him or her to use your card at all. You also have the right to advance written notice of rate increases and significant changes in terms; if you don't like the changes, you can cancel the account and pay off the balance on the current terms.

CHAPTER

9

Prepaid Cards

Until 2016, general-purpose prepaid cards were largely unregulated. In October 2016, the Consumer Financial Protection Bureau (CFPB) issued rules for prepaid cards, subjecting them to provisions similar to those for credit cards, imposing disclosure requirements, and protecting people from hidden fees, expensive credit features, and other hazards. The regulations are found in amendments to 12 C.F.R. Part 1005 (Regulation E, under Electronic Fund Transfer Act, which now covers prepaid cards as well as electronic fund transfers to and from asset accounts) and Part 1026 (Regulation Z under Truth in Lending, which now regulates credit features of prepaid cards).

The CFPB rule requires financial institutions to limit consumers' losses when funds are stolen or cards are lost, investigate and resolve errors, and give consumers free and easy access to account information, similar to provisions under the Truth in Lending Act (TILA) for credit cards and the Electronic Fund Transfer Act (EFTA) for debit cards. The CFPB also requires disclosure of fees and other key details. Finally, prepaid companies must now generally offer protections similar to those for credit cards if consumers are allowed to use credit on their accounts to pay for transactions that they lack the money to cover.

The CFPB rule covers traditional prepaid cards, including general-purpose reloadable cards. It also applies to mobile wallets, person-to-person payment products, and other electronic prepaid accounts that can store funds. Other prepaid accounts covered by the new rule include payroll cards; student financial aid disbursement cards; tax refund cards; and certain federal, state, and local government benefit cards, such as those used to distribute unemployment insurance and child support. Gift cards were already covered by the EFTA.

The rule provides that financial institutions must make certain account information available for free by telephone, online, and in writing upon request unless they provide periodic statements. Unlike checking account customers, prepaid consumers typically do not receive periodic statements by mail. The rule ensures that consumers have access to their account balances, their transaction history, and the fees they've been charged.

The rule also provides for error-resolution rights. Financial institutions must investigate claims of unauthorized or fraudulent charges or other errors on their accounts, resolve these incidents in a timely way, and restore missing funds where appropriate. If the financial institution cannot do so within a certain period of time, it will generally be required to provisionally credit the disputed amount to the consumer while it finishes its investigation.

The CFPB rule protects consumers against withdrawals, purchases, or other unauthorized transactions if their prepaid cards are lost or stolen. The rule limits consumers' liability for unauthorized charges and creates a timely way for them to get their money back. As long as the consumer promptly notifies his or her financial institution, the consumer's responsibility for any unauthorized charges will be limited to $50.

The rule also imposes disclosure requirements. The CFPB rule requires two forms, one short and one long, with easy-to-understand disclosures. The short form concisely and clearly highlights key prepaid account information, including any periodic fee, per-purchase fee, automated teller machine (ATM) withdrawal and balance inquiry fees, cash reload fee, customer service fees, and inactivity fee. The short form also must disclose certain information about additional types of fees that the consumer may be charged. Consumers will also get or be able to access the comprehensive long-form disclosure containing a complete list of fees and certain other key information before opening the account.

The rule requires prepaid account issuers to post on their websites the prepaid account agreements they offer to the general public. Additionally, with a few exceptions, issuers must submit all agreements to the CFPB, which intends to post them on a public website at a future date. Also, issuers must make any agreement not required to be posted on their websites available to applicable consumers.

The new rule includes strong protections for consumers using credit products that allow them the option of spending more money than they have deposited into the prepaid account. Under the rule, prepaid issuers must give consumers protections similar to those on credit cards if consumers are allowed to use certain linked credit products to pay for transactions that their prepaid funds would not fully cover. These protections stem mainly from the TILA and the Credit Card Accountability Responsibility and Disclosure Act (CARD) Act.

Prepaid companies, like credit card issuers, must now make sure consumers have the ability to repay the debt before offering credit. The new rule states that companies cannot open a credit card account or increase a credit line related to a prepaid card unless they consider the consumer's ability to make required payments. For consumers under the age of twenty-one, the companies will be required to assess these consumers' independent ability to repay.

Prepaid companies that provide credit have to give consumers regular statements similar to those credit card consumers receive. This statement will detail fees and, if applicable, the interest rate, what they have borrowed, how much they owe, and other key information about repaying the debt.

Prepaid companies, like credit card issuers, will be required to give consumers at least twenty-one days to repay the debt before they are charged a late fee. Late fees must also be "reasonable and proportional" to the violation of the account terms in question.

During the first year a credit account is open, total fees for credit features cannot exceed 25 percent of the credit limit. Generally, card issuers cannot hike the interest rate on an existing balance unless the cardholder has missed back-to-back payments. Card issuers may raise the interest rate in advance of new purchases, but they generally must give the consumer a forty-five-day advance notice, during which time the consumer may cancel the credit account.

The CFPB rule requires companies to wait thirty days after a consumer registers the prepaid account before offering the credit feature to the consumer. This gives consumers time to gain experience with the basic prepaid account before deciding if they want to apply for the credit feature.

Prepaid companies cannot automatically seize a credit repayment the next time a prepaid account is loaded with funds. Further, prepaid companies cannot automatically take funds from the prepaid account to repay the credit when the bill is due unless the consumer consents. And even so, companies cannot automatically take funds more than once per month. Payment also cannot be required until twenty-one days after the statement is mailed.

The effective date of the new rule was to be October 1, 2017, with the requirement for submitting agreements to the CFPB taking effect in October 2018. These dates have been postponed. How the new rule will be affected by the change in administration is unclear.

Summary

Consumer protections similar to those for credit cards are only now being implemented for general-purpose prepaid cards. Until these rules take effect, there is little in the way of protections for users of such cards.

CHAPTER

10

Debit Cards and Electronic Fund Transactions

The use of debit cards, automated teller machines (ATMs), and other electronic means to access asset accounts (checking and savings accounts) is governed by the Electronic Fund Transfer Act (EFTA) (15 U.S.C. §1693) and Consumer Financial Protection Bureau (CFPB) Regulation E (12 C.F.R. part 1005).

The statute and regulation apply to an "electronic fund transfer," which is any transfer of funds that is initiated through an electronic terminal, telephone, computer, or magnetic tape for the purpose of ordering, instructing, or authorizing a financial institution to debit or credit a consumer's account. This includes the presentation of a debit card at the point of sale, the use of an ATM, and the presentation of checks by businesses in electronic form. It does not include the writing of a check, a wire transfer, transfers for the purchase or sale of securities and commodities, transfers between accounts at a single financial institution, and single transfers initiated by telephone communications from consumers (12 C.F.R. § 1005.3).

The EFTA prohibits unauthorized issuance of debit cards and other "access devices." They can be issued to consumers only in response to an oral or written request, as a renewal of or substitution for an accepted access device (e.g., when a debit card expires), or where it cannot be used unless activated by the consumer's oral or written request, in which case the financial institution must take reasonable measures to verify that the party seeking activation is in fact the consumer (12 C.F.R. §1005.5).

The EFTA limits consumer liability for unauthorized transfers, as follows:

- A consumer has no liability unless disclosures of potential liability have been provided, the access device has been accepted, and the access device provides for a means of identifying the consumer, such as a personal identification number (PIN).
- If these conditions have been met and an unauthorized transfer or series of related transfers takes place—for example, if the debit card is stolen—the consumer's liability is not more than $50 if he or she notifies the financial institution within two business days after learning of the loss or theft.
- If the consumer fails to give notice within two business days, the limitation on liability is $500.

- If the first notice that the consumer has of an unauthorized electronic fund transfer is when it appears on a periodic statement, the consumer must notify the financial institution within sixty days of the sending of the statement to avoid liability for subsequent transfers. If the consumer fails to do so, the consumer is liable for unauthorized transfers that occur after sixty days and before notice to the institution if the institution establishes that the transaction would not have occurred had the consumer notified the institution within the sixty-day period. The period may be extended due to extenuating circumstances.
- What this means is that if a crook gains access to your account, you don't look at your monthly statements, and as a result, the person drains the account, the bank is not required to put your money back.
- It is therefore essential that consumers review bank statements carefully and notify the bank (1) if a statement is not received when it should be and (2) of any transactions that they don't recognize as proper. Notice may be given orally but should be confirmed in writing, preferably by means providing proof of receipt. (12 C.F.R. §1005.6)

These limitations are much less favorable to the consumer than those on liability for unauthorized items on credit cards. In addition, as a practical matter, "possession is nine-tenths of the law." In the case of a credit card, you have your money, and the credit card issuer must get it from you. In the case of a debit card, your money is transferred immediately, and you have to get it back if the transfer was unauthorized or there is a problem with what you purchased. Because debit cards are linked directly to your checking account, any unauthorized purchases made could put you in a real bind, depriving you of the money you need to live on. Even apart from fraud, most people have purchased something that breaks, doesn't work, doesn't fit, or otherwise is unsatisfactory. In the case of a debit card, you have been deprived of your money and have the burden of obtaining a refund, which the merchant may be slow in providing or refuse to provide at all.

Use credit cards and not debit cards for purchases of goods and services.

We therefore recommend the use of credit cards instead of debit cards for purchases of goods or services. For the same reason, we do not advise the use of debit cards or electronic fund transfers to pay debt collectors. Electronic fund transfers are appropriate to pay mortgages, car loans, and similar debts to reputable financial institutions.

Financial institutions are required to provide disclosures when a consumer contracts for electronic fund transfer services or before the first transfer is made. The disclosures include the extent of a consumer's liability, where notice of unauthorized transfers must be given, and a description of the institution's error-resolution procedures. They must also include any fees that are charged for electronic fund transfers and information on how to place a stop-payment order on such transfers (12 C.F.R. §1005.7–8).

We receive recurring complaints from consumers that creditors and debt collectors claim that recurring, or "preauthorized," electronic fund transfers cannot be canceled. This is not accurate. Any transfer can be canceled by notice to the financial institution from which the funds are to be transferred.

There are special rules for recurring electronic fund transfers. These are transfers that are scheduled to occur at regular intervals. Preauthorized electronic fund transfers must be authorized "only by a writing signed or similarly authenticated by the consumer," and the consumer must be provided with a copy by the person obtaining the authorization (12 C.F.R. §1005.10(b)). The consumer has a right to stop payment by notifying the financial institution from which the transfer is to be made orally or in writing three business days in advance of the scheduled date (12 C.F.R. §1005.10(c)). Written confirmation must normally be provided.

If the regular transfers may vary in amount, the consumer must be provided with notice of the amount at least ten days in advance of the scheduled date (12 C.F.R. §1005.10(d)).

It is illegal for any person to condition the extension of credit to the consumer on the consumer's repayment of that credit by means of electronic fund transfers, except for overdraft and similar plans (12 C.F.R. §1005.10(e)). Certain types of creditors, such as those that make high-interest "payday" and similar loans, regularly violate this prohibition.

The EFTA requires financial institutions to provide error-resolution procedures (12 C.F.R. §1005.11). Errors include unauthorized electronic fund transfers; incorrect electronic fund transfers; omission of an electronic fund transfer from a periodic statement; bookkeeping errors; incorrect amounts of money in ATM transactions; and requests for information about transfers. A financial institution must investigate and determine if an error occurred within ten business days and inform the consumer within three additional business days. If a more extensive investigation is required, the institution can take up to forty-five days if it provisionally credits the consumer's account in the amount of the alleged error within ten business days. These deadlines may be extended under limited circumstances. The institution must inform the consumer in writing of its findings and inform the consumer that he or she may obtain the documents that the institution relied on in making its determination.

Overdraft protection must be affirmatively agreed to by the consumer (12 C.F.R. § 1005.17).

Finally, the EFTA regulates remittance transfers (e.g., sending money by Western Union and similar services) and fee notices on ATMs.

Summary

The law affords you some protection against unauthorized activity involving debit cards and other electronic fund transfers, but the protection is less than provided in the case of credit cards. Use credit cards instead of debit cards for purchases of goods or services.

CHAPTER 11

Student Loan Rights

Recent student loans are not dischargeable in bankruptcy absent a strong showing of hardship. Older loans may be subject to different rules. In addition, some federal student loans are exempt from statutes of limitation. The latter depends on the program pursuant to which the loan is created and the holder of the loan (20 U.S.C. §1091a).

In the case of federally guaranteed student loans, draconian collection methods may be used that are not permitted with other debts. These include administrative wage garnishment, implemented with notice and an opportunity to object but without a court proceeding and judgment; substantial default penalties (the Department of Education allows collection costs of 25 percent or more on student loans and permits the collector to charge an amount that passes on the entire collection cost to the borrower and leaves the holder with the principal and interest owed); and interception of tax refunds and Social Security payments.

There have been rampant abuses with for-profit private schools and private student loans. For example, in February 2015 the Consumer Financial Protection Bureau (CFPB) announced a consent order with for-profit Corinthian Colleges Inc. that will forgive hundreds of millions of dollars in private student loans.

NOTE

There are around 7 million Americans currently in default of their student loan debt.

There are programs for forbearance, deferment, consolidation, and rehabilitation of federal student loans, as well as programs for repayment tied to income or that take your financial circumstances into account. There are also programs for debt forgiveness for teaching, military service, and public service work. Income-based repayment is something that will benefit many borrowers, and you should ask about it. Lenders should, but might not, volunteer the existence of such programs. In early 2017, the CFPB filed suit against Navient, a major student loan company, for steering borrowers into forbearance agreements and other expensive alternatives.

Unless specified in the loan documents, or voluntarily offered by the lender, rehabilitation programs do not apply to private loans.

Consolidation involves making a new loan that pays off the defaulted loans. Substantial fees may apply. Make certain that you understand the terms of the consolidated loan. Beware of services that offer to arrange loan consolidation for a substantial fee.

In the case of a federal loan, loan rehabilitation involves having monthly payments adjusted to an amount that is "reasonable and affordable based on the borrower's total financial circumstances" (20 U.S.C. §1078-6 (a)(1)(B)). If the borrower makes the adjusted monthly payments in a timely manner in nine of ten consecutive months, the loan is deemed to be "rehabilitated," and the prior default is removed from the borrower's credit report (20 U.S.C. §1078-6(a)(1)(A) and (C)).

Creditors, servicers, and debt collectors are obligated to notify borrowers of their rights under the federal student loan rehabilitation program. If a debt collector refuses to offer a borrower an option for which the borrower believes he or she qualifies, the borrower can ask for the Special Assistance Unit, which collectors of federal student loans are required to maintain. If that is unsuccessful, there is a Federal Student Aid Ombudsman Group at the Department of Education. In addition, misrepresentations by a debt collector about a borrower's rights under a student loan may violate the Fair Debt Collection Practices Act.

If you are faced with a collection action on a private student loan, exercise your rights as set forth in this text. In many cases, plaintiffs seeking to enforce private student loans are not the original creditors and have difficulty proving that they own or are entitled to collect the debts. Because of the size of student loans and the limited and technical nature of defenses, you should consult an attorney when faced with such action.

Summary

Be careful if you fall behind on student loans. Collection remedies are draconian and defenses few. Income-based repayment and rehabilitation should be explored in the case of federal student loans.

Other Types of Loans

Payday and Auto Title Loans

Avoid payday and auto title loans, as well as "installment" loans offered by the same establishments that make payday and auto title loans. These loans have interest rates ranging from 99 to 1000 percent and more. Although the lenders claim that you are really paying a one-time fee of $10 to $20 per $100, statistics show that very few people obtain only one high-interest loan. Rather, people repeatedly refinance loans or obtain new loans to pay off old ones, so that a borrower who gets into the payday loan trap has eight to twelve loans in one year.

Many high-interest loans are obtained over the Internet. If you have obtained one of these loans, check with your state attorney general or financial institutions regulator to see if your state requires licensing for high-interest lenders and whether your lender has a license to make loans to residents of your state. Loans made by unlicensed lenders may violate usury laws, giving rise to substantial statutory damages, or be unenforceable. In addition, attempts to collect such loans by debt collectors may violate the Fair Debt Collection Practices Act.

Some lenders claim that they are exempt from state interest regulations because they are purportedly located offshore or on Native American reservations, but courts have usually disagreed.

WARNING

Avoid payday and auto title and other high-interest loans.

Overdraft Protection

Many banks offer overdraft protection for checking accounts. They are now required to obtain your affirmative agreement to provide this.

Try to avoid overdrawing your account, and forego overdraft protection. Overdraft fees are a major source of income for banks. Many banks wait until the end of the business day and "reorder" debits so as to maximize the number of dishonored items and their overdraft fee income.

It Is Your Right to Know Why You Are Turned Down for Credit or Had Your Rate Increased

If you have been turned down for credit or granted credit at a higher rate, the Equal Credit Opportunity Act entitles you to obtain the reasons within thirty days. If a credit report was used, you must be notified which report or reports were relied on. You also have the right to a free copy of your credit report within sixty days, which you can request from the credit bureau. This is discussed in the next chapter.

Summary

Avoid high-interest loans!

Your Rights as a Debtor

According to a collections industry source, 35 percent of U.S. consumers with credit have at least one account in collections (Credit & Collection News, June 17, 2015).

The collection of consumer debts is regulated by the federal Fair Debt Collection Practices Act (FDCPA) (15 U.S.C. §1692 et seq.). The FDCPA generally applies to third-party debt collectors, which include the following:

- Collection agencies
- Collection lawyers—Lawyers were originally excluded from the definition of *debt collector*, but in 1986, Congress removed the attorney exemption, so lawyers are covered if they "regularly" collect consumer debts (*Heintz v. Jenkins*, 514 U.S. 291 (1995)). The "FDCPA does apply to a lawyer . . . with a general practice including a minor but regular practice in debt collection" (*Crossley v. Lieberman*, 90 B.R. 682, 694 (E.D.Pa. 1988), *aff'd*, 868 F.2d 566 (3d Cir. 1989)).
- Debt buyers
- Mortgage servicers that become involved with debts after they are in default (*Oppong v. First Union Mortgage Corp.*, 407 F.Supp.2d 658, 662 (E.D.Pa. 2005), *aff'd in pertinent part, vacated in part*, 215 Fed.Appx. 114 (3d Cir. 2007))
- Foreclosure lawyers, at least if they attempt to collect money or seek personal judgments (*Kaltenbach v. Richards*, 464 F.3d 524 (5th Cir. 2006); *Gburek v. Litton Loan Servicing LP*, 614 F.3d 380 (7th Cir. 2010); *Glazer v. Chase Home Finance, LLC*, 704 F.3d 453 (6th Cir. 2013); *Wallace v. Washington Mut. Bank, F.A.*, 683 F.3d 323 (6th Cir. 2012); *Reese v. Ellis, Painter, Ratterree & Adams LLP*, 678 F.3d 1211, 1217–18 (11th Cir. 2012); *Wilson v. Draper & Goldberg, P.L.L.C.*, 443 F.3d 373, 376 (4th Cir. 2006); *Brown v. Morris*, No. 04-60526, 243 Fed. Appx. 31; 2007 U.S. App. LEXIS 15396 (5th Cir., June 28, 2007) (same); *Piper v. Portnoff Law Assocs., Ltd.*, 396 F.3d 227, 233-36 (3d Cir. 2005))

- "Field agents" who work for creditors, particularly in connection with automobile and mortgage debts, and who visit consumers for the purpose of delivering communications and inducing them to communicate with the creditor (*Siwulec v. J.M. Adjustment Servs., LLC*, No. 11-2086, 2012 U.S. App. LEXIS 4201, 465 Fed.Appx. 200 (3rd Cir. March 1, 2012); *Simpson v. Safeguard Properties, L.L.C.*, No. 13 C 2453, 2013 WL 2642143 (N.D.Ill., June 12, 2013))

With a couple of exceptions, the FDCPA does not apply to original creditors. The main exception is if the creditor misrepresents that a third party has become involved in the collection process.

The FDCPA also imposes certain restrictions on professional repossessors (15 U.S.C. §1692f(6), 15 U.S.C. §1692a(6)).

The FDCPA applies to collection of a *debt*, which is defined as "any obligation or alleged obligation of a *consumer* to pay money arising out of a *transaction* in which the money, property, insurance, or services which are the subject of the transaction are primarily for *personal, family, or household purposes,* whether or not such obligation has been reduced to judgment" (emphasis added) (15 U.S.C. §1692a(5)). Debts under the FDCPA include credit card debts, mortgage debts, condominium and homeowners' association assessments, rent for a residential apartment, charges for water and sewer service originally owed to a municipality and purchased by a buyer of bad debts, and dishonored checks (even if the claim against the consumer is based on a bad-check statute rather than the contract). On the other hand, it does not include business and agricultural loans, even if incurred by an individual; liabilities for property, income, and similar taxes imposed by law rather than agreement; and liabilities for child support obligations. Tort claims by a third party with which the consumer has no contractual relationship (e.g., damages arising out of an automobile accident) are not covered because there is no "transaction." However, the fact that a claim against a consumer arising out of a transaction is phrased in terms of a statutory violation (e.g., bad-check statute) or tort (e.g., damage to a rental car may constitute the tort of negligence as well as a breach of contract) rather than breach of contract does not deprive the consumer of the protection of the FDCPA when collection agencies or collection lawyers ask the consumer to pay.

A majority of states also regulate debt collectors. The nature and scope of these restrictions vary widely. About half the states, New York City, and Buffalo, New York, impose licensing requirements. Most states impose restrictions on conduct similar to those of the FDCPA. Some state laws apply to original creditors as well as debt collectors.

The FDCPA states that its purpose is "to eliminate abusive debt collection practices by debt collectors" (15 U.S.C. §1692(e)). It applies even if there is a valid debt. The FDCPA broadly prohibits unfair or unconscionable collection methods; conduct that harasses, oppresses, or abuses any debtor; and any false, deceptive, or misleading statements in connection with the collection of a debt; it also requires debt collectors to give debtors certain information.

The FDCPA requires debt collectors to make certain affirmative disclosures to debtors. These include the following:

- Identification of debt collectors during telephone calls. 15 U.S.C. §§1692d(6) requires "meaningful disclosure" of the identity of the debt collector. This means the correct or common name of the debt-collection entity, not the real or fictitious name of the individual caller (*Edwards v. Niagara Credit Solutions, Inc.*, 586 F.Supp.2d 1346, 1352 (N.D.Ga. 2008)).

- A warning that a communication is from a debt collector and that any information provided may be used for that purpose (15 U.S.C. §1692e(11)). One reason for this requirement is to prevent debt collectors from sending people communications purporting to seek employment references, inviting the recipient to collect a prize, or otherwise disguising the true purpose of the communications (see, e.g., *Mohr v. Federal Trade Commission*, 272 F.2d 401 (9th Cir. 1959); *In re Floersheim*, 316 F.2d 423 (9th Cir. 1963)).

- A "notice of debt" containing certain information about the debt and the consumer's right to dispute it (15 U.S.C. §1692g).

Failure to make any of these disclosures constitutes a violation of the FDCPA.

The FDCPA also prohibits a wide range of conduct, falling generally into four categories: (a) improper communications with the debtor and third parties; (b) harassing, abusive, or oppressive conduct; (c) the use of false and misleading representations; and (d) the employment of unfair practices. There is substantial overlap between categories (c) and (d), particularly in the area of amounts added to the principal amount of the debt and filing or threatening lawsuits that the collector knows or should know are subject to a defense, such as the statute of limitations.

Verification of Debts

One of the most important rights conferred by the Fair Debt Collection Practices Act is the debtor's right to "validation" or "verification" of a debt (15 U.S.C. §1692g). Within five days after the initial communication with a consumer in connection with the collection of any debt, a debt collector shall, unless the following information is contained in the initial communication or the consumer has paid the debt, send the consumer a written notice containing

1. the amount of the debt;
2. the name of the creditor to whom the debt is (presently) owed;
3. a statement that unless the consumer, within thirty days after receipt of the notice, disputes the validity of the debt, or any portion thereof, the debt will be assumed to be valid by the debt collector;
4. a statement that if the consumer notifies the debt collector in writing within the thirty-day period that the debt, or any portion thereof, is disputed, the debt collector will obtain verification of the debt or a copy of a judgment against the consumer and a copy of such verification or judgment will be mailed to the consumer by the debt collector; and

5. a statement that, upon the consumer's written request within the thirty-day period, the debt collector will provide the consumer with the name and address of the original creditor, if different from the current creditor.

If the consumer notifies the debt collector in writing within the thirty-day period that the debt, or any portion thereof, is disputed, or that the consumer requests the name and address of the original creditor, the debt collector shall cease collection of the debt, or any disputed portion thereof, until the debt collector obtains verification of the debt or a copy of a judgment, or the name and address of the original creditor, and a copy of such verification or judgment, or name and address of the original creditor, is mailed to the consumer by the debt collector (15 U.S.C. §1692g(b)). The debt collector does not violate the statute if it ceases all further collection activities without providing the information. An oral dispute does not entitle the consumer to verification, but the collector cannot assume the debt is valid, and if it is reported to a credit bureau, it must be reported as disputed.

The degree of evidence necessary to constitute "verification" depends on the specificity of the dispute. A dispute stating that the debt is the result of identity theft and providing a copy of a police report or a Federal Trade Commission (FTC) identity-theft affidavit is entitled to a different response than a letter merely stating "I dispute the debt" or "I disagree with the balance claimed." The debt collector is required to fairly address any specific objection or item raised by the consumer. However, this does not require the collector or its client to agree with the consumer.

State law may give the consumer greater rights. If the debt has been sold or transferred, Section 9-406 of the Uniform Commercial Code (UCC) entitles the putative debtor to proof of the assignment. Most sales of receivables (debts) are subject to Article 9 of the UCC, dealing with secured transactions, even though they are not what normally would be thought of as a secured transaction.

State law may also give the consumer special rights in the case of identity theft (e.g., 225 ILCS 425/9.4), and many statutes regulating the extension of credit to consumers entitle a debtor to an accounting (e.g., 12 U.S.C. §2605(e) (Real Estate Settlement Procedures Act of 1974); 815 ILCS 375/15 (Motor Vehicle Retail Installment Sales Act), 815 ILCS 405/16 (Retail Installment Sales Act); 810 ILCS 5/9-210, 5/9-613 (UCC)).

The failure of a consumer to dispute the validity of a debt under the FDCPA may not be construed by any court as an admission of liability by the consumer (15 U.S.C. §1692g(c)). For example, it may not be alleged to create an account stated (*Citibank (South Dakota) N.A. v. Jones,* 184 Misc.2d 63, 706 N.Y.S.2d 301 (Nassau Cty. Dist Ct. 2000)).

Third-Party Contacts

The FDCPA provides debtors the "extremely important protection" of prohibiting debt collectors from contacting third parties, including a debtor's employer, relatives (other than the debtor's spouse), friends, or neighbors, for any purpose other than obtaining "location information" (15 U.S.C. §1692c, described in S.Rep. No. 382, 95th Cong., 2d Sess. 4, reprinted in 1977 U.S.C.C.A.N. 1695, 1698–1699). There are a few highly regulated exceptions (15 U.S.C. §1692c(b)).

Leaving messages with relatives (other than a spouse, guardian, or, in the case of a minor, parent), neighbors, credit references, employees, or coworkers is forbidden (*Horkey v. J.V.D.B. & Associates, Inc.*, 333 F.3d 769 (7th Cir. 2003) (coworkers); *West v. Costen*, 558 F.Supp. 564 (W.D.Va. 1983) (relatives)). A debt collector may not contact the superior officer of a member of the military services. Leaving a message on an answering machine or voicemail system may result in an illegal third-party communication if a third party with whom the collector could not communicate directly accesses the device or system (*Chlanda v. Wymard*, No. C-3-93-321, 1995 U.S.Dist. LEXIS 14394 (S.D. Ohio Sept. 5, 1995)).

Communications by postcard are expressly prohibited because of the risk that third parties will inadvertently see the message (15 U.S.C. §§1692b(4), 1692f(7)).

Section 1692c is violated by any communication to a third party, even if the debt is not expressly referenced, other than one that strictly complies with the provision allowing location information to be gathered. Thus, a message left with a neighbor, friend, relative, or credit reference asking to have the debtor call regarding some urgent matter is illegal (*West v. Nationwide Credit, Inc.*, 998 F.Supp. 642 (W.D.N.C. 1998)).

A debt collector may communicate with third parties for the purpose of determining the debtor's residence, telephone number, and place of employment. The debt collector must identify himself or herself and state that he or she is confirming or correcting location information concerning the debtor. The debt collector may not identify his or her employer (the collection company) unless expressly requested to do so (15 U.S.C. §1692b(1)). However, the debt collector may not state or even imply that the debtor owes a debt (15 U.S.C. §1692b(2)). The collector also cannot request more information than specified in the statute (*Shand-Pistilli v. Professional Account Services, Inc.*, 10cv1808, 2010 WL 2978029 at *4 (E.D.Pa. July 26, 2010) ("a debt collector may not seek additional information about the consumer's job including earnings information or salary, or even ask whether an individual is currently employed because such information is beyond the scope of location information")). Such a communication can be made only once unless requested by that third party or "unless the debt collector reasonably believes that the earlier response of such person is erroneous or incomplete and that such person now has correct or complete location information" (15 U.S.C. §1692b(3)). If the consumer is represented by an attorney, the debt collector may not communicate with any other person to locate the debtor. Furthermore, if the collector already has the permitted information, he or she cannot request it in order to harass the debtor. The debt collector has the burden of showing that a third-party contact was permitted.

Communication with the Debtor

The FDCPA sets out strict rules relating to communications with the debtor:

- If the debtor requests the collector to cease further communication in writing or notifies the collector in writing that he or she refuses to pay the debt, the debt collector must essentially cease all further communications (15 U.S.C. §1692c(a)). The debt collector may file a lawsuit, advise the consumer that the debt collector's further efforts are being terminated, and notify the consumer that the debt collector or creditor may invoke specified remedies that are ordinarily invoked by the debt collector or creditor or intended in the particular case. The debtor's notice is effective upon receipt, so it should be sent by fax, certified mail, or other means providing proof of receipt.

- Many people send debt collectors letters stating that they only want to be contacted in writing. This is not authorized by the statutes. Under the FDCPA, you can tell a debt collector not to contact you at work. Under another law, the Telephone Consumer Protection Act, you can tell a debt collector not to use automated equipment to call your cell phone. However, although you can insist on no further communications at all, you cannot insist that all communications be in writing.

- A debt collector may contact the debtor by phone at the debtor's residence, but only after 8:00 a.m. and before 9:00 p.m. local time at the debtor's location, unless the debtor informs the collector that another time would be more convenient (15 U.S.C. §1692c(a)(1)).

- If the debt collector knows the debtor is represented by an attorney, the debt collector may not communicate with the debtor unless the attorney consents or unless the attorney fails to respond within a reasonable time to a communication from the debt collector (15 U.S.C. §1692c(2)).

- The debtor may be contacted by phone at his or her place of employment unless the debt collector knows or has reason to know, including from a statement by the debtor, that the debtor is not permitted to receive such communication at work (15 U.S.C. §1692c(a)(3)).

- The debt collector may not communicate by postcard, and the envelope cannot bear any indication that the collector is in the debt-collection business (15 U.S.C. §§1692f(7), 1692f(8)).

- The FDCPA prohibits the placement of calls with the intent to harass the consumer (15 U.S.C. §1692d). Courts look for such matters as whether the collector threatens to continue calling after the consumer refuses to pay or states his or her inability to pay the debt, whether calls are made immediately after the consumer terminates a conversation, whether calls are made after the consumer requests that they cease, whether the content of the calls is abusive or threatening, and the volume and pattern of the calls (*Hoover v. Monarch Recovery Mgmt., Inc.*, 11cv4322, 2012 U.S. Dist. LEXIS 120948, 2012 WL 3638680 (E.D.Pa., Aug. 24, 2012); *Roth v. NCC Recovery, Inc.*, 1:10cv2569, 2012 U.S. Dist. LEXIS 101592, 2012 WL 2995456 (N.D.Ohio July 23, 2012); *Dudis v. Mary Jane M. Elliott, P.C.*, 11cv14024, 2012 U.S. Dist. LEXIS 108069, 2012 WL 3150821 (E.D.Mich., Aug. 2, 2012); *Neu v. Genpact Services, LLC*, 11cv2246, 2013 WL 1773822 (S.D.Cal., April 25, 2013)).

Special Rules Regulating Cell Phone Calls

The use of automated dialing equipment and prerecorded messages to contact debtors' cell phones is also regulated by the Telephone Consumer Protection Act (TCPA) of 1991 (47 U.S.C. §227). The TCPA and implementing regulations issued by the Federal Communications Commission require consent for automated and prerecorded calls ("robocalls") by a debt collector to a cell phone (not a landline). Providing the cell phone number as contact information to the creditor or a debt collector constitutes consent. However, consent can be revoked orally or in writing (a writing with proof of receipt is recommended for evidentiary purposes, though). There are statutory damages of $500 per call for violations, which may be trebled to $1500 if the violation is "willful."

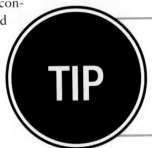

TIP

You are entitled to direct debt collectors not to robocall a cell phone. There are substantial damages for noncompliance.

Abuse and Harassment

The FDCPA prohibits a debt collector from engaging in any conduct that results in harassment, oppression, or abuse of the debtor in order to collect a debt (15 U.S.C. §1692d). Conduct that specifically is prohibited includes the use or threat of violence or criminal means, the use of abusive or profane language, and the publishing of a list of delinquent debtors (except to a consumer reporting agency). The list of prohibited conduct is not exclusive. Conduct that has been found to violate this prohibition includes threats of prohibited communications to third parties (*Rutyna v. Collection Accounts Terminal, Inc.,* 478 F.Supp. 980, 981 (N.D.Ill. 1979)), name calling, ethnic or racial slurs, derogatory remarks, and obscene and profane language (*Bingham v. Collection Bureau, Inc.,* 505 F.Supp. 864, 874 (D.N.D. 1981) (statement that debtor "should not have children if she could not afford them"); *Horkey v. J.V.D.B. & Associates, Inc.,* 333 F.3d 769 (7th Cir. 2003); *Jeter v. Credit Bureau, Inc.,* 760 F.2d 1168 (11th Cir. 1985)).

False, Misleading, and Unfair Acts and Practices

The FDCPA prohibits deceptive (15 U.S.C. §1692e) and unfair (15 U.S.C. §1692f) acts and practices in collecting debts or obtaining information about debtors. Conduct that has been found to be violative of one or both of these provisions includes the following:

- **a.** Threatening criminal prosecution when collecting bad checks, if prosecution is not legally permissible or regularly initiated (*Alger v. Ganick, O'Brien & Sarin,* 35 F.Supp.2d 148 (D.Mass. 1999); *Davis v. Commercial Check Control, Inc.,* 98 C 631, 1999 WL 89556 (N.D.Ill. Feb. 16, 1999))
- **b.** Threatening to file suit in a forum where suit cannot legally be filed (*Wiener v. Bloomfield,* 901 F.Supp. 771 (S.D.N.Y. 1995))
- **c.** Threatening to contact employers, family members, or others under circumstances prohibited by the FDCPA or other law (*Swanson v. Southern Oregon Credit Service, Inc.,* 869 F.2d 1222, 1226–27 (9th Cir. 1988))

d. Misrepresenting the legal responsibility of family members for debts (*Dutton v. Wolhar*, 809 F.Supp. 1130 (D.Del. 1992))

e. Demanding payment of a debt discharged in bankruptcy (*Turner v. J.V.D.B. & Associates, Inc.*, 330 F.3d 991 (7th Cir. 2003))

f. Obfuscating the addition of add-on expenses such as attorney's fees or collection costs (*Fields v. Wilber Law Firm, P.C.*, 383 F.3d 562 (7th Cir. 2004))

g. Seeking payment of fees and charges that are not authorized by a valid contract or by state law in the absence of a contract, such as collection charges, usurious interest, or attorney's fees where no contract or statute authorizes them (*Seeger v. AFNI, Inc.*, 548 F.3d 1107 (7th Cir. 2008) (collection charges); *In re Scrimpsher*, 17 B.R. 999 (Bankr. N.D.N.Y. 1982) (unauthorized "service charge" on NSF checks); *Pollice v. National Tax Funding, L.P.*, 225 F.3d 379, 408 (3rd Cir. 2000) ("[D]efendants presumably have violated section 1692f(1) regardless of the presence of any agreement authorizing the rates of interest and penalties, because state law specifically prohibits charging interest in excess of ten percent on the assigned claims"); *Strange v. Wexler*, 796 F.Supp. 1117 (N.D.Ill. 1992) (attorney fees); *Lox v. CDA, Ltd.*, 689 F.3d 818 (7th Cir. 2012) (attorney fees))

h. Offering to settle debts that are so old that they are beyond the statute of limitations, without disclosing that they are time-barred (*McMahon v. LVNV Funding, LLC*, 744 F.3d 1010 (7th Cir. 2014))

i. Sending letters purporting to come from an attorney, where no attorney has actually had any professional involvement with the matter, at least if that fact is not disclosed (*Clomon v. Jackson*, 988 F.2d 1314, 1321 (2d Cir. 1993); *Avila v. Rubin*, 84 F.3d 222 (7th Cir. 1996); *Nielsen v. Dickerson*, 307 F.3d 623 (7th Cir. 2002); *United States v. National Financial Services, Inc.*, 98 F.3d 131 (4th Cir. 1996); *Taylor v. Perrin, Landry, DeLaunay & Durand*, 103 F.3d 1232 (5th Cir. 1997); *Bitah v. Global Collection Servs.*, 968 F.Supp. 618 (D.N.M. 1997); *Masuda v. Thomas Richards & Co.*, 759 F.Supp. 1456, 1461-2 (C.D.Cal. 1991))

Where Collection Lawsuits May Be Filed

The FDCPA provides that debt collectors must bring suit in the judicial district or similar legal entity where the consumer signed a written contract or where the consumer resides at the time the suit is filed. In the case of an action to enforce an interest in real property securing the consumer's obligation, the action must be brought in the judicial district or similar legal entity in which the real property is located (15 U.S.C. §1692i).

Unsophisticated or Least Sophisticated Consumer Standard

Whether a debt collector's conduct violates the FDCPA is judged from the standpoint of a "least sophisticated consumer" or an "unsophisticated consumer" (*Clomon v. Jackson*, 988 F.2d 1314 (2d Cir. 1993); *Taylor v. Perrin, Landry, deLaunay & Durand*, 103 F.3d 1232 (5th Cir. 1997); *Graziano v. Harrison*, 950 F.2d 107, 111 (3d Cir. 1991). *Gammon v. GC Services Limited Partnership*, 27 F.3d 1254, 1257 (7th Cir. 1994); *McKenzie v. E.A. Uffman & Associates, Inc.*, 119 F.3d 358 (5th Cir. 1997)). The statute is liberally construed in favor of the consumer to effectuate its purposes.

Damages

The FDCPA provides for both statutory and actual damages. Statutory damages are an amount not exceeding $1000 in an individual case. In a class action, the plaintiff gets the same amount and the class an amount not exceeding the lesser of $500,000 or 1 percent of the defendant's net worth. Statutory damages are recoverable for violations, whether or not the consumer proves actual damages, and class actions are specifically authorized. It is not necessary to show that the plaintiff was actually misled by a collection notice in order to recover statutory damages (*Avila v. Rubin*, 84 F.3d 222, 227 (7th Cir. 1996); *Bartlett v. Heibl*, 128 F.3d 497 (7th Cir. 1997)). There is a short, one-year statute of limitations. A person who suffers actual damages can recover those, and the FDCPA provides for an award of attorney's fees against the defendant so that consumers do not have to pay for their own attorneys.

In addition, the FDCPA is enforced by the Consumer Financial Protection Bureau and the Federal Trade Commission.

Summary

The Fair Debt Collection Practices Act protects consumers against abusive and deceptive practices by third-party debt collectors, debt buyers, and collection lawyers, and it allows consumers to recover damages if their rights are violated.

The Collection Industry: Debt Buyers versus Original Creditors

Recent years have seen an increasing number of delinquent debts purchased by "debt buyers." Debt buyers purchase the rights to over $100 billion in the face amount of debts each year. They pay pennies on the dollar, often 3 to 4 percent of face value. If the debts are old, they may pay less than 1 percent of face value. The debt buyers then try to enforce the debts against the consumer at 100 cents on the dollar, by correspondence, telephone calls, and collection lawsuits.

Some debt buyers do their own debt collection, some use third-party debt collectors, and some do both. A majority of the debts are credit cards. Others include second mortgages, mortgage deficiencies, small loans, automobile paper, telecommunications debts, utility debts, health club debts, bank overdrafts, and medical debts.

Debt buyers pose a particularly serious problem because they rarely acquire documentation of the debts, and the information they have is often seriously inaccurate. This has been documented in a series of Federal Trade Commission (FTC) reports, one of which was based on information subpoenaed from the largest debt buyers. The agreements for the sale of charged-off debts often provide that the debts are sold "as is," without representation or warranty (see "The Structure and Practices of the Debt Buying Industry" (FTC, Jan. 2013), found at https://www.ftc.gov/sites/default/files/documents/reports/structure-and-practices-debt-buying-industry/debtbuyingreport.pdf; "Repairing a Broken System: Protecting Consumers in Debt Collection Litigation and Arbitration" (FTC, July 2010), found at https://www.ftc.gov/sites/default/files/documents/reports/federal-trade-commission-bureau-consumer-protection-staff-report-repairing-broken-system-protecting/debtcollectionreport.pdf; "Collecting Consumer Debts: The

Challenges of Change: A Federal Trade Commission Workshop Report" (FTC, Feb. 2009), found at https://www.ftc.gov/sites/default/files/documents/reports/collecting-consumer-debts-challenges-change-federal-trade-commission-workshop-report/dcwr.pdf).

Whether through inadvertence or design, debt buyers often try to collect debts from the wrong person, based on similar names and addresses. For example, in 2004, the FTC shut down a debt buyer called CAMCO. The following is from a press release issued by the FTC in connection with that case:

> . . . In papers filed with the court, the agency charged that as much as 80 percent of the money CAMCO collects comes from consumers who never owed the original debt in the first place. Many consumers pay the money to get CAMCO to stop threatening and harassing them, their families, their friends, and their co-workers.
>
> According to the FTC, CAMCO buys old debt lists that frequently contain no documentation about the original debt and in many cases no Social Security Number for the original debtor. CAMCO makes efforts to find people with the same name in the same geographic area and tries to collect the debt from them—whether or not they are the actual debtor. In papers filed with the court, the FTC alleges that CAMCO agents told consumers—even consumers who never owed the money—that they were legally obligated to pay. They told consumers that if they did not pay, CAMCO could have them arrested and jailed, seize their property, garnish their wages, and ruin their credit. All of those threats were false, according to the FTC.... (http://www.ftc.gov/opa/2004/12/camco.htm)

"Sometimes... they [debt collectors] go after people with the same names as those who owe money. They might also relentlessly call wrong phone numbers, hoping to pry information out of whoever answers. Some finagle enough identifying information to make people seem liable for debts they never owed" (Sonja Ryst, "'Debt tagging' by collection agencies a growing problem," *Washington Post*, Business section, Sunday, Aug. 8, 2010, p. G01).

The possibility that a debt buyer is suing on a debt it does not own is very real. An article that appeared in the collections industry trade press in 2007 stated:

> More collection agencies are turning to the debt resale market as a place to pick up accounts to collect on. Too small to buy portfolios directly from major credit issuers, they look to the secondary market where portfolios are resold in smaller chunks that they can handle. But what they sometimes find in the secondary market are horror stories: The same portfolio is sold to multiple buyers; the seller doesn't actually own the portfolio put up for sale; half the accounts are out of statute; accounts are rife with erroneous information; access to documentation is limited or nonexistent. (Corinna C. Petry, "Do Your Homework; Dangers Often Lay Hidden in Secondary Market Debt Portfolio Offerings. Here Are Lessons from the Market Pros That Novices Can Use to Avoid Nasty Surprises," *Collections & Credit Risk*, Mar. 2007, at 24)

A judge who regularly hears collection cases in New York noted, "[O]n a regular basis this court encounters defendants being sued on the same debt by more than one creditor alleging they are the assignee of the original credit card obligation. Often these consumers have already entered into stipulations to pay off the outstanding balance due the credit card issuer and find themselves filing an order to show cause to vacate a default judgment from an unknown debt purchaser for the same obligation" (*Chase Bank USA, N.A. v. Cardello*, 27 Misc. 3d 791, 896 N.Y.S.2d 856, 857 (Richm. Co. Civ. Ct. 2010)).

In addition, the growth of debt buying has given rise to the growth of scammers who claim to have purchased debts or to collect on behalf of debt buyers when they have no right to collect anything (Jake Halpern, "Paper Boys, Inside the Dark, Labyrinthine and Extremely Lucrative World of Consumer Debt Collection," *New York Times Magazine*, Aug. 17, 2014; Jake Halpern, *Bad Paper: Chasing Debt from Wall Street to the Underworld* (New York: Picador, 2014)).

The FTC has brought multiple enforcement actions against such scammers (http://www.ftc.gov/news-events/press-releases/2014/07/ftcs-request-court-halts-collection-allegedly-false-payday-debts; http://www.consumer.ftc.gov/articles/0258-fake-debt-collectors). The FTC has also published a warning to consumers to "be on the alert for scam artists posing as debt collectors. It may be hard to tell the difference between a legitimate debt collector and a fake one. Sometimes a fake collector may even have some of your personal information, like a bank account number" (http://www.consumer.ftc.gov/articles/0258-fake-debt-collectors). The warning advises consumers to insist on receiving a validation notice, which "must include . . . the name of the creditor you owe," and that consumers should not pay a collector who "refuses to give you all of this information." If there is any question, the consumer is instructed to contact the creditor and "find out who, if anyone, the creditor has authorized to collect the debt."

The Consumer Financial Protection Bureau (CFPB), which now has rulemaking authority with respect to the Fair Debt Collection Practices Act (FDCPA) and shares enforcement authority, has published a very similar warning (http://www.consumerfinance.gov/askcfpb/ 1699/how-can-i-verify-whether-or-not-debt-collector-legitimate.html).

In recent years, the FTC has brought at least seven proceedings against such "fake debt collectors," naming dozens of defendants.

Often, the scammers have detailed information about the debts. Sometimes they appear to have obtained the information from loan brokers that consumers may have supplied information to for the purpose of obtaining a loan. In one criminal case, a person claiming to be a prospective purchaser of debt portfolios obtained portfolio information under that pretext and then sold the information. Credit reports are another potential source of information.

A consumer cannot know, and should not assume, that a debt buyer actually owns the debt or that a debt collector is authorized to act by the true owner of the debt, even if the person contacting the consumer has information about the debts. There are many instances when a consumer pays the debt only to later receive a call—or a lawsuit—from another debt collector about the same debt. A consumer has the right to receive proof that the debt collector owns the debt or is legally entitled to collect it. Even if the consumer recognizes the debt, believes he or she owes it, and believes that the amount sought is correct, the consumer should request, at a minimum, some proof of ownership of the specific debt, such as a copy of an assignment referring to the specific debt. Otherwise, there is no guarantee that the person trying to collect the debt is not a scammer, and payment to a scammer does not satisfy the consumer's obligation. The fact that the person trying to collect the debt has fairly detailed information about the consumer or the debt does not mean that the collection attempt is authorized—the FTC and CFPB have repeatedly noted that scammers are getting such information.

Contact the original creditor and find out what happened to the debt. You may have to contact each party in the chain of title to find out what each did with the debt. Finally, contact the alleged current owner of the debt and find out whom the owner has authorized to collect it.

Do not assume that anyone who claims the right to collect a debt and has some information about you has any right to collect anything. Insist on a written "notice of debt," and verify with the original creditor whether the person contacting you is authorized to do so.

CAUTION

Summary

Many companies are in the business of acquiring charged-off consumer debts. If contacted by such a company, or by someone collecting on behalf of such a company, insist on proof that the company has the right to collect from you.

CHAPTER

15

What to Do If You Are a Defendant in a Collection Lawsuit

If you find yourself the defendant in a collection lawsuit, the first thing to do is to review and comply strictly with all deadlines and instructions in the papers you are served with. Debt collectors and collection attorneys expect that 90 percent or more of the people they sue will default and allow a judgment to be entered against them and that many of the others will simply agree to pay. Once they have a judgment, they can begin seizing assets and wages as permitted by state law. (Certain states, notably Texas and Pennsylvania, do not permit seizure of wages in most cases.)

CAUTION

If you do nothing, you lose.

Next, determine if the plaintiff is the original creditor or a debt buyer. Original creditors can often prove the debt, although there are sometimes defenses even to claims by original creditors (see following discussion). Debt buyers frequently cannot even prove that they own or have the right to collect a debt. They often follow a business model in which they file a hundred lawsuits, are able to serve ninety of the consumers, get default judgments against or settlements from eighty-five of them, and drop the cases against the five that bother to show up and defend themselves.

Get an attorney! If you are sued by a debt buyer, or if you dispute a debt with an original creditor, it is not a good idea to try to represent yourself. Laypersons are not familiar with the rules of evidence, nor are they equipped to make evidentiary objections at a trial or to determine what should be presented in a motion to dismiss or answer. Laypersons often file answers when not required or tactically desirable, making damaging admissions. We have seen many answers asserting that the creditor or debt buyer refused to work out a payment plan (generally not a defense and not properly articulated in those cases where it is, such as with some medical debt) while omitting valid defenses, such as the statute of limitations or noncompliance with laws protecting cosigners. Consult an attorney who has some experience in defending collection lawsuits.

CHAPTER 16

Defenses to Collection Claims

There are a number of substantive defenses that may exist in a collection lawsuit. Some of these are described in this chapter. Many of these issues are highly technical, and we suggest that you retain a lawyer familiar with consumer credit and debt issues to review your case and present any arguments that apply.

Bogus Charges on Credit Card Accounts

There have been a number of consent judgments and orders against major credit card issuers that involve unauthorized charges for credit insurance and similar products. The card issuers include Capital One, American Express, and Discover Bank (http://files.consumerfinance.gov/f/201207_cfpb_consent_order_0001.pdf; http://www.occ.gov/static/enforcement-actions/ea2012-212.pdf; http://files.consumerfinance.gov/f/2012-CFPB-0002-American-Express-Centurion-Consent-Order.pdf; http://www.fdic.gov/news/news/press/2012/pr12108a.pdf).

Other issuers, such as Chase and General Electric/Synchrony/CareCredit, have been involved in litigation that casts serious doubt on the accuracy of their records and the validity of the accounts (Consumer Financial Protection Bureau (CFPB) consent orders 2013-CFPB-0007 (Chase) and 2015-CFPB-0013 (Chase); Office of the Comptroller of the Currency consent orders AA-EC-13-76 (Chase) and AA-EC-2014-64 (Chase); CFPB consent order 2013-CFPB-0009 (CareCredit)). If a credit card account involved one of these issuers, and especially if the facts of your case resemble the conduct at issue in the prior cases, it may be very hard for the issuer, or anyone claiming to have acquired the debt from the issuer, to prove anything.

Capacity of Parties to Credit Card Accounts

Generally, "authorized users" of a credit card are not personally liable; only the cardholder is. If two names appear on a monthly credit card statement and it is disputed who is a signatory and who is the authorized user, the bank or debt buyer cannot prevail without proving who is a signatory. This issue often arises after death, divorce, or bankruptcy of one of the two. Banks often have poor records and cannot prove this, and often they do not transfer such records that they do have to debt buyers. It appears that many banks keep applications or images of applications for not more than seven years after the account is opened (not after the account is closed).

Statutes of Limitations

All states limit the time within which a lawsuit may be filed by private parties on various types of debts. (Sometimes there are no time limitations on debts owed to governmental entities.)

Statute of limitations periods vary from one to fifteen years. Common variations are the type of debt and the extent to which the debt has been reduced to writing. For example, most states have a four-year statute of limitations in the Uniform Commercial Code for debts arising out of the sale or lease of goods (automobiles, fuel oil, natural gas). Often, there are special statutes of limitation for dishonored checks and penalties under bad-check statutes. The statutes generally run from the later of breach or last payment, although the effect of payments varies between states.

In addition, some states will look to the limitations provisions in other states to determine whether a debt is time-barred. For example, New York looks to the state in which the creditor is located (*Portfolio Recovery Associates, LLC v. King*, 14 N.Y.3d 410, 901 N.Y.S.2d 575, 927 N.E.2d 1059 (2010)). Some states will apply the law of another state if there is a choice of law provision in a contract, which is common with credit card agreements. Other states have "borrowing" statutes so that if a consumer defaults on a debt while residing in state A and later moves to state B with a longer statute of limitations, a court in state B may apply the shorter limitations provision of state A.

Filing suit on a time-barred debt not only gives rise to a defense but is a violation of the Fair Debt Collection Practices Act (FDCPA) (*Phillips v. Asset Acceptance, LLC*, 736 F.3d 1076, 1079 (7th Cir. 2013)). Threatening to file suit on a time-barred debt is also an FDCPA violation. An increasing number of courts hold that a debt collector seeking to

> **NOTE**
>
> Do not assume that if a lawyer files a lawsuit that he or she has the right to do so. Debt buyers and collection attorneys often ignore statutes of limitations, hoping that the consumer will default and a judgment will be entered even though the consumer has a complete defense to the claim.

collect a time-barred debt who implies that the debt is legally enforceable—such as by offering a settlement—must disclose that the debt is time-barred (*McMahon v. LVNV Funding, LLC*, 744 F.3d 1010 (7th Cir. 2014)). Some states have passed statutes or issued regulations requiring debt collectors to make this disclosure whenever attempting to collect time-barred debts.

Promises to Answer for the Debt of Another

Virtually all states have one or more "statutes of frauds." These laws require a signed writing before a person can be held liable for certain types of debts. One type of debt commonly covered by statutes of frauds is a promise to answer for the debt of another.

There are differences between states as to exactly what debts are covered and whether the debt has to already exist when the promise to pay it is made. This issue commonly arises when persons are added to credit card accounts and with claims by nursing homes against relatives of patients.

Liability of Parents and Spouses

Under American common law (judge-made law), a parent is liable for the "necessaries" of an unemancipated minor child, and a husband is liable for the "necessaries" of a wife. Various states have modified the liability of spouses by statute or case law. In community property states, debts may be the responsibility of both spouses. Some non-community-property states have abolished spousal liability for necessaries. Others have made the obligation applicable to both husband and wife, or limited liability for "necessaries" to cases where the noncontracting spouse has a materially greater ability to pay. In addition, the doctrine of necessaries has been codified or expanded by statute in some states (e.g., Illinois Family Expense Act, 750 ILCS 65/15).

A further complication is introduced by the federal Equal Credit Opportunity Act (ECOA), which arguably precludes the use of all such statutes and rules of law to impose personal liability on a noncontracting spouse where a creditor obtains the obligation of only one spouse on a contract involving the extension of credit (deferral of payment). The ECOA and implementing Regulation B entitles each spouse to contract to purchase goods or services on their own, without the agreement or participation of the other (15 U.S.C. §1691d; 12 C.F.R. §1002.7). It expressly preempts (overrides) state laws that provide lesser rights (12 C.F.R. §1002.11).

The ECOA is presently administered by the CFPB. Previously, when it was administered by the Federal Reserve Board, that agency issued a statement that "in States that have laws prohibiting separate extensions of credit for married persons, this section of the regulation will not only preempt such laws but *also any other provision of State laws which would hold one spouse responsible for the debts contracted by the other, for example, a family expense statute*" (emphasis added) (40 Fed. Reg. 49298, at 49304 (Oct. 22, 1975)).

If a spouse or parent is liable for a debt based on one of these rules, the liability is generally for the reasonable value of goods or services. Liability may or may not extend to contractual undertakings to pay attorney's fees, collection costs, late fees, interest, and similar items.

Attempts to collect debts from the family members of a deceased consumer who have no legal liability are a widespread problem. The Federal Trade Commission (FTC) published a statement on such attempts, "Statement of Policy Regarding Communications in Connection with the Collection of Decedents' Debts" (76 Fed. Reg. 44915 (Wed., July 27, 2011)). People assume that someone has to pay the debt; this is not the case.

Liability of Children for Parent's Debts

Generally, in the United States a child has no responsibility for the debts of a parent. However, a few states have "filial responsibility statutes," meaning that adult children are required to pay at least some of the unpaid medical bills of a parent when the estate can't. In 2012, such statutes existed in Alaska, California, Connecticut, Delaware, Georgia, Indiana, Iowa, Kentucky, Louisiana, Maryland, Massachusetts, Mississippi, Montana, Nevada, New Hampshire, New Jersey, North Carolina, North Dakota, Ohio, Oregon, Pennsylvania, Rhode Island, South Dakota, Tennessee, Utah, Vermont, Virginia, West Virginia, and Puerto Rico.

These laws vary widely in terms of what debts are covered and who can enforce them (some are limited to medical assistance provided by state or local government). There are substantial issues as to the validity of such statutes under the ECOA and otherwise.

Nursing Home Debts

Attempts to collect from family members are particularly common in the case of nursing home debts. Often, a family member will sign a contract with a nursing home as an agent of the resident. Notwithstanding contract claims by nursing homes, such a signature generally does not impose any personal obligation on the family member. The principal is the only party to a contract signed by an agent who discloses both that he or she is signing as agent and who the principal is. The statute of frauds (see previous discussion) may also prevent the imposition of liability on an agent who clearly signs as such.

In addition, nursing homes that accept Medicare or Medicaid payments for any patient are precluded from requiring a guaranty from anyone other than the resident by federal law as a condition of admission or continued stay at a nursing home (42 U.S.C. §1396r(c)(5)(A)(ii)). The prohibition is not limited to the specific patients for whom Medicare or Medicaid payments are received. The exact meaning of the prohibition is unclear—does it merely prohibit refusing to keep the resident in the nursing home, or does it prohibit trying to hold the relative liable? The prohibition should also extend to the use of the "necessaries" doctrine and family expense statutes to impose liability amounting to a guaranty.

Other Health-Care Debts

Collection suits for healthcare debts are difficult to prove. Absent an express agreement to perform a particular service for a specific price, as is occasionally done for elective procedures (e.g., cosmetic surgery), the patient is liable for the reasonable cost of medically necessary services (e.g., *Dreyer Medical Clinic v. Corral*, 227 Ill.App. 3d 221, 591 N.E.2d 111 (2d Dist. 1992)). This is generally not something the patient can know, and it is not easy to prove if contested.

NOTE

Most hospital bills contain both billing errors and items that are priced far beyond their cost. Proving that all items in a hospital bill were both reasonable and medically necessary is not easy.

At the outset, beware of attempts to charge for items for which the hospital has contractually agreed not to charge. Many insurance policies and plans require the provider to accept whatever the insurer pays for a given procedure. The Medicaid and Medicare statutes have parallel restrictions. Check the "explanation of benefits" from the insurer for the required contractual write-off, and compare the medical bill to see if you are being improperly "balance billed" for amounts the provider is required to write off.

Some providers will decline to process charges through an insurance plan if they believe that they can get more through other means. This is common where the patient has been injured as the result of an accident; the hospital thinks it can get more by placing a lien on the patient's tort recovery. Many contracts between hospitals and insurers forbid this practice by requiring the hospital to submit a claim for any patient who presents an insurance card. If you believe this has happened, complain to the insurer. In many cases, the insurer is advancing money to the hospital based on expected revenues. If the hospital removes from the pipeline cases where it thinks it can obtain more from a lien, it is cheating the insurer as well as violating the patient's rights.

TIP

You should request an itemized copy of the medical bill.

Usually, patients are initially sent a summarized version of the hospital bill. However, an itemized bill is likely to reveal some obvious errors. For example, compare the dates noted on the bill with the dates you actually received treatment. Look for absurd data-entry errors such as numbers with zeros added on (e.g., ten X-rays) or duplicate listings. Do you remember receiving the services listed?

Obtain a copy of your medical chart and pharmacy ledger (which shows all drugs administered). Compare it to the itemized hospital bill. This may reveal whether you are being charged for goods or services that were not furnished. Look for mistakes such as procedures billed for but not in the medical record, items billed for more times than listed in the medical record, procedures or medications ordered but canceled, and operating room time that is billed for longer than the surgery lasted.

Compare the charges to the hospital's standard charges. These are usually in a document called a "chargemaster."

Look for items improperly billed due to the hospital's negligence. We had a case where a surgical implement was incorrectly left in the patient, requiring surgery for its removal, and the hospital sued the patient for the cost of the corrective surgery! If the results of a test are misplaced and the procedure is redone, the hospital may bill the patient. Complications that result from negligence, such as staph infections, should not be the patient's responsibility. Longer hospital stays resulting from scheduling problems should not be the patient's responsibility.

If the bill is large, there are professional bill reviewers who look for errors in bills. For example, a procedure may be given a code ("DRG code") that reflects a more serious condition than what the medical chart states. Other DRG codes are supposed to include a "bundle" of charges, some of which may also be billed separately. Inquire about possible alternative codes that could have been assigned and the cost implications. Also inquire whether the hospital has ever been charged with miscoding or inappropriate coding by any governmental agency or insurance company.

Finally, the reasonableness of a hospital's rates is often subject to challenge. Uninsured persons generally are charged more to make up for lower rates of reimbursement offered by the government or private insurance providers.

To a growing extent, medical debts are being sold to debt buyers. It should be evident from the previous discussion that it is highly unlikely that a debt buyer who does not have access to hospital/provider witnesses can ever prove a medical debt.

Some consumer advocates have suggested that patients pay a small portion of the bill as a sign of good faith while trying to negotiate payments with a hospital. *We strongly recommend that you do not do anything of the sort, as such a payment may be treated as an admission of the validity of the entire debt.* If it is an older debt, making a payment may extend the statute of limitations.

Generally, a consumer should not make a payment on a disputed debt without a satisfactory written agreement completely resolving the matter upon the completion of specified payments.

> **WARNING**
>
> If you do not agree you owe a debt in full, in the amount claimed, do not make partial payments. Dispute the debt. Otherwise, you will make damaging admissions and will extend the time within which you may be sued.

If you agree to pay a sum and make monthly payments, the agreement should address whether the debt is bearing interest. A proper settlement agreement will state that the consumer will make x payments of $\$y$ each and that upon completion of those payments, all liability on the part of the consumer is released. You should also attempt to address credit reporting in the agreement.

The federal Patient Protection and Affordable Care Act (Obamacare) and Treasury regulations issued in final form on December 29, 2014, limit non-profit hospitals from engaging in "extraordinary collection actions" (26 C.F.R. §1.501(r) et seq.). Hospitals cannot file lawsuits against patients or put liens on their houses before determining whether they are eligible for financial assistance. "Extraordinary collection actions" also include selling debts to debt buyers, reporting adverse information about the individual to consumer credit reporting agencies or credit bureaus, requiring a payment before providing medically necessary care, and any legal or judicial process.

Some states have similar restrictions. In addition, some states regulate the amount that uninsured patients can be charged and require that payment plans be offered on hospital bills (this is an unusual requirement—with the exception of medical debts and mortgages, in most cases a creditor is not obligated to offer a payment plan).

It is often a good idea to request a jury trial in a hospital collection case. It is hard to find a juror who has not had a negative experience with healthcare costs.

Automobile Deficiencies

Under the Uniform Commercial Code (UCC), in effect in virtually all states, a creditor or assignee attempting to collect on a deficiency after repossession of a car or other collateral has to prove that proper notice was given and that there was a "commercially reasonable" disposition of the collateral. Major auto creditors can sometimes prove that they complied with these requirements. Smaller creditors often don't comply, and debt buyers that claim to acquire this type of debt generally can't prove that the original creditor complied.

Additional requirements are often imposed by state installment sales and consumer protection laws. These requirements include bars on deficiencies, requirements of pre-repossession notice, requirements that cosigners be allowed to take over the debt before any collection action is taken, requirements that consumers be allowed to reinstate contracts if they have paid over a certain percentage of the debt, and others.

In addition to constituting a defense to liability, noncompliance with the UCC or other requirements often gives rise to a claim for substantial statutory damages against the creditor or assignee. For example, the UCC provision applicable to consumer cases provides for statutory damages equal to the finance charge (whether or not paid) plus 10 percent of the amount financed or cash price.

Defects in the goods (e.g., lemon cars) may often be asserted against the finance company. An FTC regulation subjects the holder or assignee of a note or retail installment contract to claims or defenses that a consumer has against the seller of the goods or services financed if the seller was involved in the origination of the financing obligation or the referral of the consumer to the finance company.

Finally, in many states there is a separate UCC statute of limitations for claims for nonpayment for the sale or lease of goods (four years). It may be extended by payment or, in some cases, promises to pay.

A consumer faced with such a case should consult a local attorney familiar with these matters. They are not something that a layperson should attempt to raise on his or her own.

Defective Goods and Services

Earlier, we pointed out that, with certain exceptions, the fact that goods and services purchased with a credit card are defective may be asserted as a defense against the credit card issuer. This is just one aspect of a general principle that one who purchases a debt takes subject to claims against the creditor prior to assignment. "The rule is that the assignee of a contract takes it subject to the defenses which existed against the assignor at the time of the assignment" (*Allis-Chalmers Credit Corp. v. McCormick*, 30 Ill.App.3d 423, 424, 331 N.E.2d 832 (4th Dist. 1975); *accord, Montgomery Ward & Co. v. Wetzel*, 98 Ill.App.3d 243, 423 N.E.2d 1170, 1175 (1st Dist. 1981) ("the assignee thus takes the assignor's interest subject to all legal and equitable defenses existing at the time of assignment")). For example, in a collection action based on a contract for the purchase of a car, the defendant can assert that the car was defective.

Summary

There are numerous defenses to various types of debt-collection actions. The issues are complicated, and we strongly advise hiring a lawyer to review and defend any debt-collection lawsuit.

Dealing with Collection Calls

What to Say and What Not to Say

Because of the prevalence of abusive and scam debt collectors and the theft of information via hacking and similar means, a consumer should never agree to pay a debt based solely on a telephone call. You should beware of any debt collectors that demand immediate payment or request that you provide bank account information over the phone.

Such demands are often coupled with baseless threats of arrest, lawsuits, and the like. Demands and threats of this nature are indicative of scams. Even if you receive a call from someone purporting to represent the original creditor, if you do not personally recognize the caller, call the company back at a number you obtain from a bill or the Internet.

Beware of fake debt collectors, which often have obtained information about your debts through various means.

If you are dealing with a debt collector or debt buyer, you have the right to a written "notice of debt" stating who currently owns the debt. If the original creditor owns the debt, call the creditor and ask who, if anyone, the original creditor has authorized to collect the debt. If it is not the original creditor, call the original creditor and inquire whom the company sold the debt to. You may have to contact successive purchasers until you get to the current owner of the debt. Contact that party, and make sure that the person attempting to collect the debt is authorized to do so.

Do not ignore collection letters or calls if you do not recognize the debt. Attempts to collect money from the wrong person through calls, letters, or even lawsuits are common. This can result from error (finding the wrong person through "skip tracing," "mixed-file" issues on the part of credit bureaus, etc.), fraud on the part of the debt collector (see the CAMCO case, described in a previous chapter), or identity theft. The problem is especially serious when people have similar names, either because they are related (e.g., Jr./Sr.) or because they have common names. It should be addressed as early as possible, before the collector files a lawsuit. Send a letter documenting the fact that you are not the person who owes the money. Make sure you keep a copy. We suggest using means that provides proof of receipt. Individuals who are subjected to collection efforts on a debt belonging to someone else should also obtain all three of their credit reports and make sure that there is no information on them that is not theirs.

How to End Harassing Telephone Calls

Under the Fair Debt Collection Practices Act (FDCPA), a consumer has an absolute right to instruct a debt collector to cease contact (15 U.S.C. §1692c). This right must be exercised in writing and is effective upon receipt, so we suggest using a method of notice that produces proof of receipt (fax, certified mail, overnight mail).

The FDCPA does *not* give a consumer the right to insist that all communications be in writing. It does allow a consumer to inform a debt collector that telephone communications are at "a time or place known or which should be known to be inconvenient to the consumer" (15 U.S.C. §1692c(a)(1)). Absent some unusual circumstances, such as a consumer's medical condition, this probably does *not* allow a consumer to insist that all communications be in writing. It would, for example, allow a consumer who works a night shift to instruct the collector not to contact him during ordinarily permissible daylight hours if that is when the consumer sleeps.

The FDCPA also provides that communications may not be sent to "the consumer's place of employment if the debt collector knows or has reason to know that the consumer's employer prohibits the consumer from receiving such communication" (15 U.S.C. §1692c(a)(3)). The source of knowledge may be the consumer.

Under a different federal statute, the Telephone Consumer Protection Act (TCPA), a consumer has the right to direct that a debt collector cannot use automated telephone-dialing equipment to place calls or text messages to the consumer's *cell phone* (47 U.S.C. §227). The TCPA contains a general prohibition against the use of automated telephone-dialing equipment or a recorded or computer-generated voice to call cell phones. There is no restriction on debt-collection calls (as opposed to telemarketing or advertising calls) to landlines if the consumer is not charged for the call. The Federal Communications Commission (FCC), which administers the TCPA, has ruled that (1) consumers who provide their cell numbers to a creditor or debt collector consent to being robocalled at the number provided, but (2) a consumer may revoke consent by notice (*In the Matter of Rules and Regulations Implementing the Telephone Consumer Protection Act of 1991; Request of ACA International for Clarification and Declaratory Ruling*, CG Docket No. 02-278, FCC Release 07-232, 23 FCC Rcd 559, 565, 2008 WL 65485; 43 Comm. Reg. (P & F) 877 (Jan. 4, 2008); *In the Matter of Rules and Regulations Implementing the Telephone Consumer Protection Act of 1991, American Association of Healthcare Administrative Management, Petition for Expedited Declaratory Ruling and Exemption*, CG Docket No. 02-278, WC Docket No. 07-135, FCC Release 15-72 30 FCC Rcd. 7961, 62 Comm. Reg. (P & F) 1539, 2015 WL 4387780 (July 10, 2015)). Notice may be given orally, although for purposes of proof, it is obviously better to use a writing.

Although you can direct a debt collector not to contact you, this does not extinguish any liability you have or prevent the debt collector from filing a lawsuit.

Negotiating a Payback Arrangement

Both original creditors and debt buyers will generally agree to settle debts or accept payment plans. If you are not dealing directly with an original creditor, first make certain that the person you are dealing with is authorized to act on behalf of the owner of the debt, as pointed out previously.

Generally, a consumer should not make a payment on a disputed debt without a satisfactory written agreement completely resolving the matter upon the completion of specified payments. If you agree to pay a sum and make monthly payments, the agreement should address whether the debt is bearing interest. A proper settlement agreement will state that the consumer will make x payments of $\$y$ each and that upon completion of those payments, all liability on the part of the consumer is released. You should also attempt to address credit reporting in the agreement.

TIP

If you do not have sufficient funds to deal with all of your debts, deal first with those claims that you are less likely to be able to defend against. This would include recent debts held by the original creditors with respect to which you don't have any substantive defenses. The extent to which a debt collector is harassing you should not be a consideration.

Consumer credit counseling services (nonprofit) can be of assistance in this regard. Conversely, stay away from companies that want to charge you a percentage of what they can "save" you on a debt.

When to Contact a Lawyer Regarding Debt Collection

Consult an attorney if you:

- Are being harassed or abused by a debt collector;
- Receive collection letters or calls on debts that you are having difficulty paying;

- Receive collection letters or calls that you do not understand or do not agree with;
- Receive collection letters or calls that appear to be trying to collect a debt owed by someone else and you cannot get them to stop immediately;
- Are being bombarded by robocalls; or
- Are named as a defendant in a collection lawsuit.

Summary

You have the right to direct a debt collector to cease contact with you. You should not respond to collection calls demanding immediate action until verification of the debt has been provided to you.

CHAPTER

18

Credit and Spending: Avoiding Common Mistakes and Borrowing Responsibly

The following are some tips for the responsible use of credit:

- Shop around for credit. If you cannot get credit at a reasonable rate, consider whether you should get it at all. If you have to pay over 30 percent for credit, something is wrong.
- Do not get credit without a clear plan as to how you are going to repay it. Obtaining another extension of credit is not such a plan. That is how people get into the "payday loan debt trap."
- Do not ignore credit problems. Generally, credit problems get worse when left alone. It is in your best interest to directly address any such problems as quickly as possible. One of the most common responses to a financial crisis, such as a job loss, is to continue spending at the same level using credit cards. This is not a good idea. It typically takes a job seeker one month to replace $10,000 of lost income.
- If you have saved money for retirement, do *not* use it in a financial crisis, at least in a state that protects such assets from seizure by creditors. Taking cash out of a traditional individual retirement account (IRA) can lead to a 10 percent penalty and taxes of at least 25 percent if the person is younger than 59-1/2 years old. There are exceptions, such as if the withdrawal is made to pay

for medical expenses. However, even apart from the exceptions, you are always going to need financial reserves, even if the crisis leads you to bankruptcy. We strongly suggest that consumers *never* pay creditors with assets that a creditor cannot reach by legal process.

- Get organized. Make payments on time. The easiest way to damage your credit score is to make late payments. Just one missed payment could drop your score significantly. Either enroll in automatic payment programs or develop a system that works for you and reminds you when bills are due. One easy system is to pay outstanding bills with approaching due dates on the immediately preceding payday.

- Stay in control. Develop a budget. Collect your bills. Write down your recurring monthly expenses in four categories: (1) essential fixed payments, such as housing, car payments, insurance, and minimum payments on credit cards; (2) essential nonfixed expenses, such as food, gas, utilities, and medical expenses; (3) discretionary expenses, such as clothing and entertainment and savings; and (4) expenses that you should try to eliminate (tobacco, alcohol).

  Then keep to the budget. Without discipline, impulse control, and diligent logging of your income and expenses, a budget does no good. All members of the household need to participate in this. Save receipts so you can tell if you are keeping to your budget.

  Determine the amount you can afford to save each month. Have it direct-deposited into a savings account or mutual fund. Over time, it will make a big difference. Being able to put money down on a car or home will result in substantially lower payments and interest costs.

- Do not max out credit cards or lines of credit. Excess "utilization" of available credit brings down your credit score. Try to keep your utilization rate (credit balances divided by your credit limits) between 1 and 20 percent. To lower your utilization rate, try making payments more than once a month, asking for a credit limit increase, or simply using your cards less.

- If you find that you are carrying balances on credit cards from month to month, identify the card with the highest interest rate and pay as much as you can each month, while paying the minimum balance on other cards, until it is paid off. Then, choose the next card and pay extra on it while you pay minimums on the others. If you pay only the minimums on all your cards, you'll be paying a lot more in interest than you may realize.

- Avoid impulse purchases of substantial items. The fact that something is on sale is not a reason to purchase it if you don't need it or cannot afford it.

- Use cash instead of credit or debit cards for discretionary spending. Take out enough cash to last one to two weeks at a time. Make up your mind that the cash you have is all you get for discretionary expenses, or things that you could live without, each week. It's much easier to turn down a $100 pair of shoes when it will take the last of your week's cash than it is when you just have to swipe a credit card.

- Avoid useless expenses like overdraft charges. Balance your checkbook regularly, and reconcile your checkbook with your bank statements. If your bank gives you free checking if you keep a certain sum of money in the account, keep the money there without using it. If you're on a tight budget, a couple of small mistakes can lead to overdraft charges and insufficient funds in your account.
- Do not apply for excessive amounts of credit. Every time you apply for a new credit account, the lender will pull your credit report and add a hard inquiry. In addition, having excess credit may tempt you to use it.
- Not using any credit is also a mistake. Lenders actually like seeing consumers responsibly use credit. You can't prove that you're a responsible user of credit without using credit. Also, if you don't use your credit cards, your lenders may close your accounts, which could further hurt your score. Instead, use your cards for modest purchases and pay off the balance the same month or the next month.
- Don't be quick to cosign or guarantee debts of others. One of the most frequent inquiries we receive is from cosigners and is "How can I remove myself from X's debt. X isn't making payments, and it is harming my credit." X is often a former significant other.

    In most cases, the answer is that you can't. The entire reason creditors want cosigners is that they don't trust the primary debtor to repay the debt, so they want someone more creditworthy—the cosigner—to be liable for it.

    This raises the following question. Creditors have credit scoring models and lots of experience in evaluating whether consumers will repay their debts. They request cosigners because they do not trust that the person applying for credit will repay it. If an experienced professional creditor with far more expertise in evaluating credit risks doesn't trust the person applying for credit to repay it, doesn't that tell you something?

    There may be times when you want to cosign anyway. Your child may need a first loan, or a close friend may need help. Before you do so, consider carefully how it might affect your financial well-being.

- Can you afford to pay the loan? If you're asked to pay and can't, you could be sued or your credit rating could be damaged.
- Even if you're not asked to repay the debt, your liability for the loan must be disclosed on your credit applications and may keep you from getting other credit. Creditors will consider the cosigned loan as one of your obligations.
- Before you pledge property to secure the loan, make sure you understand the consequences. If the borrower defaults, you could lose these items.
- Obtain a copy of the Truth in Lending Act disclosures concerning the loan so that you know the amount you might owe.
- You may be able to negotiate specific terms of your obligation. For example, you may want to limit your liability to the principal on the loan and not include late charges, court costs, or attorney's fees or limit your liability to a specific amount. This must be in the loan document and signed.

• Insist that the loan document (this must be in writing) provide that any creditor or subsequent holder must notify you if the borrower misses a payment or (very important) requests forbearance or an extension or other change in terms. Many form loan documents provide that the bank can change the terms or grant forbearances or extensions without affecting the cosigner's liability. That sort of provision should be deleted and replaced with the one described. That will give you time to deal with the problem without affecting your credit, or to make back payments without having to repay the entire amount immediately. Such notice is mandated under the laws of some states, but not everywhere (e.g., 815 ILCS 505/2S). If provided for by contract, the creditor or holder will be required to comply before you can be held liable.

In sum, cosigning a debt may well amount to a gift in the amount of the debt to the person you are cosigning for. If you are not comfortable with the idea of such a gift, don't cosign.

If you already have cosigned or guaranteed a debt, the law does afford a number of protections. First, under the "statutes of frauds" in force in most states, agreements to pay the debt of another generally must be in writing, signed by the party to be charged with liability. There is no such thing as an oral guaranty.

Second, the guaranty may not be valid. There are special notice requirements imposed by Federal Trade Commission regulations (16 C.F.R. §444.3) and also by laws in many states. Noncompliance may invalidate the guaranty.

Other states require a written notice to the cosigner or guarantor before collection action is taken so that the cosigner may take over payments and protect his or her credit (e.g., 815 ILCS 505/2S).

Finally, there is an extensive body of law on whether extensions and forbearances by the creditor to the principal debtor release the cosigner. Most standard-form bank documents attempt to reserve the right on the part of the bank to grant such extensions without releasing the cosigner.

• Make sure it is in writing.

All agreements with banks and creditors need to be (1) in writing, (2) signed by the bank or creditor, and (3) made part of the basic note, guarantee, or other credit instrument.

WARNING

All agreements with banks and creditors need to be (1) in writing, (2) signed by the bank or creditor, and (3) made part of the basic note, guarantee, or other credit instrument. Agreements that do not meet all three requirements may not be enforceable.

Apart from the general principle that oral agreements are worth the paper they are written on (nothing) and the propensity of certain creditors (such as car dealers) to dispute or deny oral agreements, most states have statutes of frauds that make certain promises legally unenforceable unless in writing, signed by the party to be charged with a promise. This is a pre-1776 English law that was widely adopted in the United States.

Common statutes of frauds require signed writings for promises relating to the transfer of an interest in real estate (including a mortgage), promises that are not to be performed or are not by their terms capable of performance within one year (exactly what contracts are covered varies), and promises relating to the sale of goods for more than $500. If a writing is required and does not exist, the party seeking to enforce the promise loses.

In addition, at the insistence of the banking industry, many states have enacted special statutes of frauds that protect banks, credit unions, and other professional lenders by making some or all promises relating to the extension of credit unenforceable unless they are in writing, signed by a bank officer. Some of these laws are limited to commercial loans, whereas some extend to all loans (e.g., 815 ILCS 160/1 et seq.).

Finally, if a bank fails and is taken over by state or federal regulators, federal law provides that even written promises by a federally insured institution that are not part of the basic loan instrument are generally not binding (*D'Oench, Duhme & Co. v. Federal Deposit Ins. Corp.*, 315 U.S. 447 (1942), codified and expanded upon at 12 U.S.C. §1823(e)). Even a *signed* "side agreement" purporting to alter the terms of what appears to be an unconditional note or loan agreement will not bind the regulator or someone who acquires the loan from the regulator. All agreements must be in the same document that creates the obligation.

The theory behind this rather harsh rule is that bank examiners need to be able to rely on what they find in the bank's loan files in carrying out their duties, and allowing such hidden agreements, oral or written, would operate as a fraud on the system of bank regulation and insurance. A bank customer cannot agree with a friendly or corrupt bank officer outside of the loan document because what appears to be a valid note in the bank's files and carried on the bank's books at face value is really a worthless piece of paper that will not be enforced against the customer. Given the number of major banks that have failed (e.g., Washington Mutual, Indymac), this is a serious problem.

Your Rights with Respect to Credit Reports

If you've ever applied for a charge account, a personal loan, insurance, or a job, someone is probably keeping a file on you. This file might contain information on how you pay your bills or whether you've been sued, arrested, or have filed for bankruptcy.

Companies that gather and sell this information are called consumer reporting agencies or credit bureaus. The information sold by consumer reporting agencies to creditors, employers, insurers, and other businesses is called a consumer report. The most familiar types of consumer reports generally contain information about where you work and live and about your bill-paying habits. Other, less well-known reports containing information about your banking activities, relationships with landlords, medical history, criminal history, and insurance claim and litigation history that are used to evaluate you for credit or employment are also "consumer reports," and you are entitled to the same legal protections for these reports.

Congress created a law that gives consumers specific rights in dealing with consumer reporting agencies. The Fair Credit Reporting Act (FCRA) (15 U.S.C. §1681 et seq.) protects you by requiring that consumer reporting agencies furnish correct and complete information to businesses for use in evaluating your application for credit, insurance, or a job.

Under the FCRA:

- You have the right to have your performance on credit obligations reported accurately by credit bureaus if it is reported at all. Contrary to popular belief, there is no legal requirement that creditors report to credit bureaus unless they promise you to do so in a contract.

- You have the right to be informed if information on your credit file has been used against you, to either deny credit or insurance or increase the cost of credit or insurance. If you applied for and were denied credit, or the cost of credit was increased, the Equal Credit Opportunity Act (ECOA) requires the creditor to tell you the specific reasons for the decision. For example, the creditor must tell you whether the denial was because you have "no credit file" with a consumer reporting agency or because the consumer reporting agency says you have "delinquent obligations." This law also requires that creditors consider, upon your request, additional information you might supply about your credit history.

- You have the right to know what is in your credit file and to receive a free credit report from each consumer reporting agency (credit bureau) once per year.
- You have the right to ask for your credit score.
- You have the right to dispute incomplete or inaccurate or obsolete information in your credit file.
- You have the right to have your credit file used only for specified permissible purposes.

These rights apply with respect to a number of different types of consumer reporting agencies:

- The three major national credit bureaus—Experian, Equifax, and TransUnion;
- The far more numerous consumer reporting agencies that collect information about how you handle your bank accounts, your insurance claims, and other aspects of your life—for example, ChexSystems and Early Warning collect information about bank account activity (unpaid overdrafts, accounts closed for suspected fraud, etc.), and TeleCheck and Certegy maintain information about dishonored checks for retailers;
- Agencies that perform screening for prospective employers and landlords, generally obtaining information about prior evictions and litigation, criminal background, and other personal information;
- Agencies that prepare "merged" reports for mortgage and other lenders, and
- Specialized consumer reporting agencies that report on "subprime" transactions.

A consumer reporting agency subject to the FCRA includes "any person which, for monetary fees, dues, or on a cooperative nonprofit basis, regularly engages in whole or in part in the practice of assembling or evaluating consumer credit information or other information on consumers for the purpose of furnishing consumer reports to third parties and which uses any means or facility of interstate commerce for the purpose of preparing or furnishing consumer reports." A "consumer report" is "any written, oral, or other communication of any information by a consumer reporting agency bearing on a consumer's creditworthiness, credit standing, credit capacity, character, general reputation, personal characteristics, or mode of living which is used or expected to be used or collected in whole or in part for the purpose of serving as a factor in establishing the consumer's eligibility for—(A) credit or insurance to be used primarily for personal, family, or household purposes; (B) employment purposes; or (C) any other purpose authorized under section 1681b of this title" (15 U.S.C. §1681a).

Credit Scores and How They Are Calculated

Approximately 90 percent of credit scoring relating to extensions of credit in the United States uses a methodology developed by the Fair Isaac Corporation (FICO). The remainder uses a similar methodology developed by VantageScore (used by Experian and TransUnion) and PLUS Score (Experian). Insurance companies use a similar "credit-based insurance score" in setting auto and home-owner premiums.

FICO scores vary between 300 and 850. Most people score in the 600s and 700s. Most lenders consider scores above 750 to be excellent, 700 good, 650 fair, and anything under 600 poor, resulting in credit denial or subprime rates.

The actual formula or algorithm used by FICO is nonpublic, and there are some forty or fifty variations on the FICO score (a 2012 report from the Consumer Financial Protection Bureau puts the number at forty-nine). FICO has different models tailored to the loan product the consumer applies for and creates custom scores for its clients.

In addition, FICO has changed its general formulas over the years. For example, in 2014, the company announced FICO 9, its newest version of the basic algorithm. FICO 9 does not include paid collection accounts in its scoring system and counts medical debt differently than other debts because medical debt is often an unplanned expense beyond the consumer's control.

Generally, however, approximately 35 percent of any FICO score is based on credit history, 30 percent on the amounts owed, 10 percent on whether the consumer has recently applied for credit, 15 percent on length of credit history, and 10 percent on the types of credit used by the consumer. For particular groups, such as people with short credit histories, the relative importance of these categories may be different (http://www.myfico.com/crediteducation/whatsinyourscore.aspx).

In order to have a credit score, it is generally necessary to have at least one credit account active for a minimum of six months or to have had credit activity within the past six months. The most recent models expand this to twenty-four months, allowing an additional 30 to 35 million consumers to have credit scores.

A FICO score is calculated each time it is requested, based on the information that is on your credit report at that time. Because Equifax, Experian, and TransUnion have similar but not identical information about a consumer, the corresponding FICO scores will also differ slightly. Substantial differences between the credit scores suggest a problem with the information retrieved by one or more bureaus.

Some prospective creditors check all three scores. This is common for mortgage companies. Some auto lenders or credit card companies may only check one.

Many websites offer generic or "educational" credit scores that are not FICO scores. You should be aware of exactly what you are purchasing before agreeing to pay money for a credit score.

Credit History

Credit history includes late payments on credit cards, charge accounts, installment loans, finance company accounts, and mortgage loans; collection items;

and public records such as judgments, bankruptcies, foreclosures, and liens. Older and smaller items are less serious than recent and larger items. Chapter 13 bankruptcies are not given more favorable treatment than Chapter 7s.

Whether you have recently opened or applied for accounts makes up approximately 10 percent of your credit score, generally with a negative impact.

Having a long credit history is favorable and accounts for approximately 15 percent of your credit score.

Having a mix of different types of credit, such as credit cards and installment loans (mortgage, auto credit) is normal and adds to your score.

Amounts Owed

Amounts owed includes the absolute amount owed, how many accounts have balances, "utilization" (the percentage of a person's available credit that is used), and the extent to which installment obligations have been paid down. Having a very small balance without missing a payment may be slightly better than carrying no balance at all.

Closing unused credit accounts that have zero balances and are in good standing will not raise your FICO score. It may actually harm it because closing an account reduces the amount of available credit you have, and as a result, your credit utilization will go up.

Generally, utilizing more than 50 percent of total available credit may adversely impact one's credit score. FICO maintains that people who max out credit cards are more likely to miss future payments, and therefore the FICO score considers people using more of their available credit to be more risky than people who are using very little of their available credit.

Closing a credit account will *not* result in deletion of the "tradeline" (the information relating to an account on a credit report).

What Credit Scores Do Not Consider

FICO scores do not consider race, color, religion, national origin, sex or marital status, age, salary, occupation or employment history, address, or child/family support obligations. FICO scores also do not consider the exercise of rights under federal consumer protection laws, including the exercise of your right to obtain your own credit report or credit score (assuming this is done as a consumer request and not by having someone with access to the credit report "pull" it).

FICO scores do not expressly consider the annual percentage rates charged on particular accounts. However, because FICO does consider the balances outstanding and the proportion of available credit that is used, and because payments on a higher-APR obligation reduce the balance less than payments on a low-APR obligation, paying higher-APR obligations has a more favorable impact on credit scores than paying lower-APR obligations.

FICO scores are issued to an individual, so each spouse/partner has his or her own.

Effect of Credit Inquiries on Credit Score

Some but not all credit inquiries affect your FICO score. Certain types of "soft" inquiries do not count—consumers who request their own credit reports, requests by credit grantors made for promotional purposes, requests made by existing creditors for purposes of reviewing your account, and requests by employers or prospective employers. Only "hard" inquiries—inquiries where a potential lender is reviewing your credit because you've applied for credit with the lender—are counted.

The information about inquiries that can be factored into your FICO score includes the number of recent credit inquiries and the time since the credit inquiries. The extent to which inquiries affect your credit score varies. For many people, one additional credit inquiry has no impact. For others, it takes less than 5 points off the FICO score. Inquiries can have a greater impact, however, if you have few accounts or a short credit history. Large numbers of inquiries also mean greater risk.

Multiple inquiries relating to a mortgage loan, auto loan, student loan, or apartment rental application within a period of thirty to forty-five days are treated as a single inquiry so that consumers are not penalized for shopping for the best rates and terms. On the other hand, each inquiry relating to an application for a credit card or an increased balance on an existing credit card is considered a separate inquiry. FICO claims that persons with six or more inquiries on their credit reports are eight times more likely to declare bankruptcy than people with no inquiries on their reports.

Participation in credit counseling does not count.

Improving Your Credit Score

It is not possible to quickly improve one's FICO score. Beware of companies claiming that they can do this. In the past, people have claimed that your credit can be quickly fixed by creating a new identity using a taxpayer identification number instead of a Social Security number or by paying people to list you as an authorized user on existing accounts. Such attempts are fraudulent and may result in substantial civil and criminal liability. Also, creditors and FICO have adopted measures to catch such attempts.

Beware of companies that want money to improve your credit score.

Improving credit scores takes time. Absent erroneous or outdated information on your credit report (see following discussion), the best way is to pay debts down regularly over time. Many banks offer payment reminders or automatic payments, in which you are either reminded to make a payment or the payment is made automatically. If you have multiple credit card accounts, pay down the ones with the highest annual percentage rate (APR) first, while maintaining your other

Closing an account doesn't make it go away.

accounts in current status. Do not close accounts, including unused accounts. Owing the same amount of money but having fewer open accounts may actually lower a FICO score because higher utilization of accounts is a negative factor. However, do not open new credit card accounts that you do not need because lowering the average account age is a negative factor. Someone with no credit cards, for example, tends to be a higher risk than someone who has managed credit cards responsibly.

Paying Off Collection Accounts

After a debt is delinquent, it is "charged off" and may be sent to collections. "Charging off" a debt does not affect the consumer's liability. It is an account-

"Charging off" a debt does not mean it cannot be collected.

ing term that means that the debt can no longer be listed on the books of a business as a valid receivable, worth 100 cents on the dollar. Federally insured financial institutions are generally required to charge off open-end credit accounts (such as credit cards) when they are 180 days delinquent and closed-end accounts (such as loans or retail installment contracts) when they are 120 days delinquent.

This is required to prevent banks from creating a false impression of financial soundness. The consumer is not let off the hook.

If you pay a debt that has been charged off and sent to collections, you are *not* entitled to have it removed from your credit report or credit score. Some creditors will agree to do this, which is desirable. Whether such an agreement is legally enforceable is not clear.

You are entitled to have the item listed as paid. The outstanding balance on a paid collection item should be changed to zero. How quickly that will happen depends on when the collection agency provides the updated information to the credit bureaus. If the company doesn't, you can and should dispute the collection account directly with the credit reporting agencies.

Under most credit scoring models used as of June 2015, paying a collection item will not significantly increase your credit score. Collection accounts are considered negative, whether paid or unpaid.

However, VantageScore 3, the most recent version of a credit scoring model used by some lenders, disregards collection accounts where the balance is zero.

FICO 9, the newest version of the FICO score, will also disregard collection accounts where the balance is zero. However, it could be a significant amount of time before FICO 9 is widely adopted by lenders.

It should be noted that some lenders, especially mortgage and auto lenders, will insist that unpaid collection accounts be resolved before they will extend credit.

Foreclosures and Foreclosure Alternatives

FICO states that it treats foreclosure alternatives involving something other than "paid as agreed"—short sales, deeds-in-lieu of foreclosure, consent foreclosures—the same as a foreclosure for credit scoring. One alternative may be better for a consumer legally or financially but not for credit scoring purposes. A sale of the property for an amount sufficient to pay the loan off will have a lesser impact, even if preceded by late or missing payments.

The impact of a foreclosure or foreclosure alternative lessens over time. If a consumer keeps all other credit obligations in good standing, the FICO score will begin to improve in about two years.

Cleaning Up Errors on Your Credit Report

You are entitled to one free credit report from each bureau each year.

Approximately one-third of credit reports issued by the three major national credit bureaus have significant errors in them. The extent of errors in the reports of other credit bureaus is even greater.

You are entitled under federal law to one free credit report from each bureau per year. Some states, such as California, give you the right to additional reports. You are also entitled under federal law to a free credit report if you have been the subject of "adverse action"—denial or higher-than-optimal pricing of credit—based on the report and you make the request within sixty days. You are also entitled under federal law to one free report once in any twelve-month period if you certify in writing that you

- Are unemployed and intend to apply for a job in the next sixty days;
- Are receiving public welfare assistance; or
- Believe that your report is wrong due to fraud.

If you don't meet one of these requirements and do not live in a state that entitles you to additional free credit reports, the consumer reporting agency may charge a reasonable fee, probably around $10.

The consumer reporting agency is required to give you all the information in your report and, in most cases, the sources of that information. You also have the right to be told upon request the name of anyone who received a report on you in the past twelve months, and you may also request the address and phone number of each such person or company. (If your inquiry concerns a job application, you can get the names of those who received a report during the past two years.) The consumer reporting agency must also provide you with a written summary of your rights under the FCRA.

We strongly recommend that you obtain your free annual credit reports. Requesting one every four months is a good idea. This is the address:

Annual Credit Report Request Service
P.O. Box 105281
Atlanta, GA 30348-5281
877-322-8228
www.annualcreditreport.com

You have to provide your name, address (last two years), Social Security number, and date of birth. You may be asked to provide proof of your identity.

The free credit report generally does not include your credit score. These can be purchased:

www.myfico.com
866-406-7204

You do get a free credit score when applying for a mortgage or home equity loan.

What Types of Information on Your Credit Report May Be Challenged

When you get your credit reports, review them carefully, looking for any information that does not belong to you—including address and other information that is not a part of a "tradeline." The presence of information that does not belong to you indicates either identity theft or a "mixed-file" problem.

Identity theft involves someone fraudulently obtaining credit, employment, medical treatment, or other benefits using your name or identifying information.

A "mixed-file" problem arises from the fact that the credit bureaus use "algorithms" to identify people with information that do not require 100 percent matching of name, address, and Social Security numbers, so that a request for information pertaining to A pulls up information about B because B has similar but not identical identifiers.

Sometimes consumers who are victims of mixed files will mistakenly believe they are the victim of identity theft, and the credit bureaus themselves will sometimes request that they follow identity-theft procedures when the problem is really a mixed file. You should consider the possibility of a mixed file if the other person involved has the same or a similar name and/or a Social Security number that is close to your number. The credit bureaus' algorithms for matching information with individuals are not the same, so a file may be mixed by one bureau but not others.

Certain common situations often give rise to mixed-file problems. Persons whose names are the same except for "Junior," "Senior," or the like frequently have their files mixed. The similarity of names plus a common current or past address may trigger a credit bureau's matching algorithms. Family members who immigrate to the United States at the same time and have similar names may have their files mixed. They may be issued Social Security numbers that differ by only one digit; that plus the similarity of names and a common address at one time may trigger a credit bureau's matching algorithms.

You should also look for "obsolete" information. Generally, information may remain on your credit report for the following periods:

1. Bankruptcy filings—ten years;
2. Civil suits, civil judgments, and records of arrest—seven years or until the governing statute of limitations has expired, whichever is longer; note that in some states, judgments can be enforced for twenty to thirty years;
3. Paid tax liens—seven years from date of payment (there may not be any limit on unpaid tax liens);
4. Accounts placed for collection or "charged off"—seven years; the seven years begins 180 days after the date of the commencement of the delinquency that immediately preceded the collection activity, charge to profit and loss, or similar action; the seven years is not extended by payment;
5. Any other adverse item of information, other than records of convictions of crimes—seven years;
6. Information on a report generated because of an application for a job with a salary of more than $75,000—no time limitation; and
7. Information on a report generated because of an application for more than $150,000 worth of credit or life insurance—no time limitation.

We have found that some debt-collection agencies attempt to change the date of last activity in order to keep items on people's credit reports past the seven-year limit (a process known as "re-aging"). This is a violation of the Fair Debt Collection Practices Act.

Finally, some information on credit reports is often incorrect. This may be the result of errors by either the furnisher of information or the credit bureau itself. Incorrect information about late payments and the like is usually the result of furnisher error. Credit bureaus also make errors, such as misreporting information from public court records—for example, reporting a judgment in someone's favor as a judgment against them.

If you find any information on your credit reports that does not belong to you or is not accurate or is obsolete, you should *write* to the bureau in question (we suggest a letter rather than online disputes), retaining a copy of what you send. *Oral complaints are not sufficient to preserve your legal rights.*

WARNING

Incorrect "tradelines" on your credit reports must be disputed in writing with the credit bureaus, not just the furnishers of the information.

You should do this not only for "tradelines"—reports of the extension of credit—that are not yours but for *any* incorrect information, including name and address and employment information. If the information concerns a "tradeline," send a copy of the letter to the furnisher of information. However—and this is very important—*communications solely with the furnisher of information do not preserve your rights under the FCRA.* Furthermore, several federal courts have decided that the FCRA preempts all or most claims of any sort based on the furnishing of incorrect information by a merchant to a credit bureau, so that if you do not preserve your rights under the FCRA, you may not have any other rights (*Purcell v. Bank of America*, 659 F.3d 622 (7th Cir. 2011) (court held that the FCRA preempts all state law claims such as defamation, even if willful and malicious); *Macpherson v. JP Morgan Chase Bank, NA*, 665 F.3d 45 (2d Cir. 2011) (same)). Also, if a dispute was required, you cannot recover damages that were suffered prior to the time the dispute process was completed.

The credit bureau has thirty days to investigate after receiving a dispute, which normally includes contacting the source of information, and correct the information. If the creditor or other source of information furnishes false information to the consumer reporting agency in response to its inquiry, you have the right to sue the creditor.

Be as specific as possible. The agency is required to delete or reinvestigate the items in question. If the new investigation reveals an error, a corrected consumer report will be sent to you, and upon your request, to anyone who received your report in the past six months (job applicants can have corrected reports sent to anyone who received a copy during the past two years).

Keep copies of your dispute correspondence, copies of your credit reports, and a log of any other communications with the credit bureaus. Do not discard old credit reports—the credit bureaus often do not keep, or claim not to keep, copies of reports they have issued. Also keep copies of all documents proving that the information you are disputing is indeed inaccurate. Finally, keep all documents proving you have suffered damages as a result of the errors, such as letters turning you down for credit, notices of interest-rate hikes resulting from derogatory credit items, medical bills for stress-related ailments, and so forth. If you have been turned down for credit due to errors, they should write down the date, whom they spoke with, exactly what they said, which credit bureau they relied on, and any other relevant information.

If you dispute the accuracy of the information in your file and the consumer reporting agency deletes it, the agency cannot put the disputed information back into your file without notifying you in writing. This requirement is often not honored because the furnisher submits the same information again and the agency does not catch it.

If the investigation does not resolve your dispute, you have the right to have the consumer reporting agency include your version of the disputed information in your file and in future reports. You may submit a written statement of any length to be included in your file, although if the consumer reporting agency helps consumers write a clear summary of the dispute, the statement may be limited to one hundred words. At your request, the consumer reporting agency will also show your version or a summary of your version to anyone who recently received a copy of the old report. There is no charge for this service if it's requested within thirty days after you receive notice of your application denial. After that, there may be a reasonable charge.

Some "credit repair organizations" and Internet sources will suggest that you submit disputes about any negative information on a credit report, even if accurate and not obsolete, on the theory that the information has to be removed if the furnisher does not verify it in time. This is *not* a good idea. ***You do not have a legal right to remove current, accurate information from a credit report.*** Furthermore, if some information is obsolete or inaccurate, a pattern of submitting bogus disputes destroys your credibility and makes it harder to deal with information that you have a right to remove.

WARNING

Disputing negative information on your credit report that is accurate and within the applicable time limits is not a good idea.

Credit bureaus have the right to reject disputes as "frivolous" or "irrelevant." Generally, they will do this when they believe that they are receiving disputes from a credit repair organization or where they receive repeated disputes concerning the same item of information, particularly disputes that do not articulate what is wrong with the report.

Under a March 9, 2015, consent agreement with the State of New York, the three major credit bureaus were required to use trained employees to review the documentation consumers submit when they believe there is an error in their files. If a creditor says its information is correct, an employee at the credit reporting firm must still look into it and resolve the dispute.

Under the same agreement, credit reporting firms will have to wait 180 days before adding any information about medical debt to consumers' credit reports. When medical debts are paid by an insurance company or benefits provider, regardless of the time frame, they will have to be removed from the credit report soon after. This avoids penalizing consumers who have medical coverage but are involved in disputes with the insurance company or other benefits provider.

A similar but more extensive agreement with thirty-one states was announced on May 20, 2015. Under this agreement, the three major bureaus are required to:

- Improve the dispute-resolution process so that consumers who find errors on their credit reports can get them easily corrected.
- Provide consistent standards to data furnishers, keep a list of companies that routinely report bad or inaccurate credit information to the agencies, and provide that list to the attorneys general. This will allow the states to go after "furnishers" that report faulty information.
- Stop pitching credit monitoring services or other fee-based products to consumers who call with complaints until the agencies have resolved the consumers' problems.
- Pay the states $6 million for the cost of the investigation.
- Improve their dispute-resolution processes so that consumers can have their issues investigated.
- Promote the website where consumers can get free credit reports.
- Wait 180 days before placing derogatory medical debts on a credit report.

The reason for the focus on medical debt is that it is a significant credit reporting problem. Approximately 20 percent of all persons with credit reports—about 43 million people—had a collection item on the report relating to a medical bill. More than half of all collection items on credit reports are medical bills. The average size of the bills is only about $200. Over 20 percent of consumers with collection items on their credit reports have only medical collection items. In many cases, the medical collection item results from the failure of medical providers or insurance companies to properly submit and pay a medical claim rather than the inability of the patient to pay. At the same time, a medical collection item can cause a one-hundred-point drop in a credit score.

Who Can Get My Credit Report?

A credit report can only be given to those with certain specified permissible purposes.

However, in most cases involving the proposed granting of credit or the proposed issuance of insurance or an application for an apartment, you do *not* have to be told or consent before someone asks for a report. (This is commonly misunderstood; we receive lots of complaints that "someone pulled my credit without my permission.") A company may request a consumer report without telling you *if* the company has reasonable grounds to believe that it will engage in a transaction with you to which your creditworthiness is relevant. For example, if you visit a car dealer and ask about buying a car on time, the dealer has the right to run a credit report. But if you just ask about buying a car, it doesn't. Offering to pay by personal check probably entitles the recipient to obtain your credit report, however.

A consumer reporting agency may not provide a consumer report to an employer or prospective employer unless the employer has your written permission. Also, your written permission is needed before medical information may be reported by a consumer reporting agency for credit, insurance, or employment purposes.

Some states make it illegal for employers to require a credit check on job applicants unless the job falls into one of the exceptions—primarily jobs that involve the handling of over a certain amount of cash or that grant access to customers' personal financial information. In addition, federal law creates additional exceptions (for federal employees and persons working for federally chartered or regulated financial institutions and in national-security-related positions). These restrictions apply only to conventional credit reports and not to background checks concerning such matters as criminal histories.

Are Reports Prepared on Insurance and Job Applicants Different?

If a report is prepared on you in response to an insurance or job application, it may be an investigative consumer report. These are much more detailed than regular consumer reports. They often involve interviews with acquaintances about your lifestyle, character, and reputation. Unlike regular consumer reports, you'll be notified in writing when a company orders an investigative report about you. This notice will also explain your right to ask for additional information about the report from the company you applied to, or you may prefer to obtain a complete disclosure by contacting the consumer reporting agency. Note that the consumer reporting agency does not have to reveal the sources of the investigative information.

If an employer or prospective employer intends to take any adverse action against you based on a consumer report, whether or not it is an investigative consumer report, the employer must first—before the adverse action is taken—give you a copy of your report and a summary of your rights under the federal FCRA and afford you an opportunity to dispute erroneous information. This requirement is often not complied with.

Tenant Screening

Tenant screening reports are becoming more of a problem. Some landlords are blacklisting tenants who have been involved in litigation with landlords, regardless of who filed it or the outcome. Some landlords have policies of refusing to rent to all individuals who have had an eviction filed against them, with no exceptions (such as that it was filed in error and dismissed or resulted from a mortgage foreclosure or homeowners' association action against the prior landlord in which the tenant was named because he or she was a tenant, even though the tenant paid the rent). Although the tenant screening entities are covered by the FCRA, the problem is that the information they are relying on may be accurate.

In some states, the court files relating to eviction actions against tenants who are not found by a court to have been delinquent on their rent (either because they were not alleged to be delinquent or because their position was found to be meritorious) are sealed and cannot legally be reported. In addition, refusing to extend credit because of the good-faith exercise of rights under various consumer protection laws may be illegal.

Generally, landlords are not required to inform a prospective tenant that they intend to obtain information from a tenant screening service. An application for a rental—the request for credit—is the only "permission" necessary to obtain a report. The law does not require that the consumer be informed of the service unless the report is used to deny a lease, increase the price, or impose other conditions, such as a cosigner, in which case the applicant must be given an "adverse action notice" identifying the source of the report. A few cities and states do require advance notice. For example, New York City requires advance disclosure of any consumer reporting agency used to evaluate the application.

Employment Background Checks

There are far more background screening agencies than there are credit bureaus, and they seem to be much sloppier than the credit bureaus. Criminal background information does not always include Social Security numbers or a physical description, so people with common names may have all kinds of information erroneously included in their reports. We have seen information included in criminal background check reports that obviously could not pertain to the job applicant, such as a conviction of a person who was serving a long prison sentence at the time the applicant was interviewed (a fact readily ascertainable from the correctional authorities) or was obviously not of the same race as the applicant.

Employers and prospective employers must obtain permission to do a background check in writing, and there are strict rules about what the form must look like. The FCRA requires that before obtaining a background or credit check on an applicant or employee, an employer must give the individual a "clear and conspicuous" written disclosure that a consumer report is being obtained for employment purposes. The document should consist solely of that disclosure. The form cannot contain extraneous information, such as a liability release or an at-will employment disclaimer.

The FCRA also requires that before taking an adverse action (such as not hiring an applicant) based in whole or in part on information obtained from a consumer report, an employer must provide the individual with a copy of the report and a government-prescribed summary of the consumer's rights under the FCRA. The employer must then give the individual a reasonable amount of time to dispute the accuracy of the information before proceeding with the adverse action. If adverse action is taken, a second notice is required.

State laws prohibiting employers from obtaining credit checks on prospective employees do not prohibit background checks, although both types of reports are "consumer reports" covered by the FCRA.

List of Tenant and Employment Screening Agencies

The Consumer Financial Protection Bureau (CFPB) maintains a list of consumer reporting agencies at http://files.consumerfinance.gov/f/201604_cfpb_list-of-consumer-reporting-companies.pdf

Summary

It is important that you understand and monitor your credit reports and credit score.

Improving Your Credit Score

It is not possible to quickly improve one's credit score. You should beware of people claiming that they can do this—such promises are generally "too good to be true." In the past, people have claimed that your credit can be quickly fixed by creating a new identity using a taxpayer identification number instead of a Social Security number or by paying unrelated people to list you as an authorized user on existing accounts with a good payment history. Such attempts are fraudulent and may result in substantial civil and criminal liability, especially if you obtain credit through such means and then default.

For example, presenting a credit application that does not disclose your liabilities may make the debt nondischargeable in bankruptcy. Presenting a credit application to a financial institution (directly or through a dealer or retailer) that is known to contain materially false information is generally criminal.

Also, creditors and the Fair Isaac Corporation (FICO) have adopted measures to catch such attempts, so they are not likely to succeed.

Generally, improving your credit scores takes time. Absent erroneous or outdated information on your credit report, the best way is to pay debts down regularly over time. Many banks offer payment reminders or automatic payments, in which you are either reminded to make a payment or the payment is made automatically. If you have multiple credit card accounts, pay down the ones with the highest annual percentage rate (APR) first while maintaining your other accounts in current status. Do not close accounts, including unused accounts, because owing the same amount of money but having fewer open accounts may actually

Closing an account doesn't make it go away.

If you encounter financial distress, the worst thing you can do is not deal with it.

lower a FICO score—higher utilization of accounts is a negative factor. However, do not open new credit card accounts that you do not need because lowering the average account age is a negative factor. Someone with no credit cards, for example, tends to be a higher risk than someone who has managed credit cards responsibly.

First, determine what expenses are essential, at least at some level, and which are not. Utility bills can be reduced, but the basic minimum should be treated as essential.

Try to pay at least the minimums on all of your credit cards. If that is not possible, and you expect the financial distress to be temporary, contact the creditors and negotiate terms. Particularly if the account has been in good standing for a long time, creditors are often willing to do this.

One reason creditors are willing to negotiate is that they do not want to "charge off" accounts if they can avoid doing so. Creditors that are public companies or insured financial institutions are subject to reporting requirements enforced by the Securities and Exchange Commission and banking regulators. Generally, federally insured financial institutions must remove ("charge off") accounts from the asset side of their balance sheets when they are 120 days (closed-end or installment credit) or 180 days (open-end credit, such as credit cards) delinquent.

Generally, after filing either a Chapter 7 or a Chapter 13 bankruptcy, credit will not be readily available to you—at least at reasonable rates—for about two years.

After bankruptcy, make sure that your prebankruptcy debts—other than those that are reaffirmed—are reporting on your credit report as discharged, with a zero balance. This is how they are legally required to be reported, but sometimes they are not.

People sometimes refer to not "including" debts in a bankruptcy. There is no such thing. You are legally required to list all of your assets and debts on a bankruptcy petition and schedules. In a Chapter 7, all scheduled debts are discharged. If there are no assets, debts that are not scheduled may also be discharged, depending on the jurisdiction.

In some cases, a debt may be "reaffirmed." In other cases, a creditor may permit you to continue making payments on a secured debt (car loan, home mortgage) without foreclosing or repossessing, even though your personal liability is extinguished. Consult a bankruptcy attorney before doing either.

Try to pay all of your postbankruptcy and reaffirmed debts on time. After a couple of years, your credit score will begin to recover.

After the bankruptcy, begin reestablishing your credit as soon as possible. One possibility is to obtain a secured credit card. This type of credit card typically includes a credit limit equal to an amount that you have deposited with the card issuer. Make sure the card issuer reports your payments to the credit bureaus.

Summary

Improving your credit score requires time and effort. There are no quick fixes.

When to Hire a Lawyer to Deal with a Credit Report Problem

If you think your legal rights have been violated by (a) a consumer reporting agency, (b) a person furnishing information to a consumer reporting agency, or (c) a person using information from a consumer reporting agency (including an employer), you should seek the advice of an attorney. In some cases, but not always, a consumer reporting agency or other person who has violated the Fair Credit Reporting Act (FCRA) must pay damages and your attorney's fee. You generally have **two years** in which to bring suit.

There are two principal obligations imposed by the FCRA in cases of inaccurate information. First, the bureaus are required to "follow reasonable procedures to assure **maximum possible accuracy** of the information concerning the individual about whom the report relates" (emphasis added) (15 U.S.C. §1681e(b)). This section is most appropriate for situations that are clearly the credit bureau's fault—such as a mixed-file case or the misreporting of public record information. The algorithms used to "match" files may not satisfy this standard.

Under another section of the FCRA, there is an obligation to conduct a reasonable investigation if you dispute an item; 15 U.S.C. §1681i, "Procedure in case of disputed accuracy," states:

a. Reinvestigations of disputed information.

    1. Reinvestigation required.

        A. In general. If the completeness or accuracy of any item of information contained in a consumer's file at a consumer reporting agency is disputed by the consumer and the consumer notifies the agency directly of such dispute, the agency shall reinvestigate free of charge and record the current status of the disputed information, or delete the item from the file in accordance with paragraph (5), before the end of the 30-day period beginning on the date on which the agency receives the notice of the dispute from the consumer.

   B. Extension of period to reinvestigate. Except as provided in subparagraph (C), the 30-day period described in subparagraph (A) may be extended for not more than 15 additional days if the consumer reporting agency receives information from the consumer during that 30-day period that is relevant to the reinvestigation.

   C. Limitations on extension of period to reinvestigate. Subparagraph (B) shall not apply to any reinvestigation in which, during the 30-day period described in subparagraph (A), the information that is the subject of the reinvestigation is found to be inaccurate or incomplete or the consumer reporting agency determines that the information cannot be verified.

2. Prompt notice of dispute to furnisher of information.

   A. In general. Before the expiration of the 5-business-day period beginning on the date on which a consumer reporting agency receives notice of a dispute from any consumer in accordance with paragraph (1), the agency shall provide notification of the dispute to any person who provided any item of information in dispute, at the address and in the manner established with the person. The notice shall include all relevant information regarding the dispute that the agency has received from the consumer.

   B. Provision of other information from consumer. The consumer reporting agency shall promptly provide to the person who provided the information in dispute all relevant information regarding the dispute that is received by the agency from the consumer after the period referred to in subparagraph (A) and before the end of the period referred to in paragraph (1)(A). . . .

3. Consideration of consumer information. In conducting any reinvestigation under paragraph (1) with respect to disputed information in the file of any consumer, the consumer reporting agency shall review and consider all relevant information submitted by the consumer in the period described in paragraph (1)(A) with respect to such disputed information.

4. Treatment of inaccurate or unverifiable information.

   A. In general. If, after any reinvestigation under paragraph (1) of any information disputed by a consumer, an item of the information is found to be inaccurate or incomplete or cannot be verified, the consumer reporting agency shall promptly delete that item of information from the consumer's file or modify that item of information, as appropriate, based on the results of the reinvestigation. . . .

The obligation to investigate is imposed on both the bureau and the furnisher of information. The bureau must take reasonable measures to initiate an investigation. If information from a furnisher is involved, it must take reasonable measures to communicate the dispute to the furnisher. The furnisher must, upon receipt of a dispute from the bureau (not directly), conduct a reasonable investigation and accurately report its results to the bureau. The bureau must act reasonably in evaluating the response.

A reasonable investigation generally does not extend to resolving contested issues of fact or law relating to a dispute between the furnisher and the consumer, although the "tradeline" must be listed as disputed.

Claims against furnishers of information are generally dependent on the consumer disputing with the bureau first. Although furnishers also have a duty to report accurate information, there is usually no private right of action by a consumer for failure to do so, absent a dispute with the bureau. You can copy the furnisher on your letter to the bureau, but it is absolutely essential to give notice to the credit bureau in order to take legal action against anyone for failure to investigate a dispute. Only government agencies can pursue a furnisher without a dispute through the bureaus.

This somewhat counterintuitive scheme is created by 15 U.S.C. §1681s-2(b), which provides:

b. Duties of furnishers of information upon notice of dispute.

1. In general. After receiving notice pursuant to section 611(a)(2) [15 USC §1681i(a)(2)] of a dispute with regard to the completeness or accuracy of any information provided by a person to a consumer reporting agency, the person shall

   A. conduct an investigation with respect to the disputed information;

   B. review all relevant information provided by the consumer reporting agency pursuant to section 611(a)(2) [15 USC §1681i(a)(2)];

   C. report the results of the investigation to the consumer reporting agency; and

   D. if the investigation finds that the information is incomplete or inaccurate, report those results to all other consumer reporting agencies to which the person furnished the information and that compile and maintain files on consumers on a nationwide basis.

   E. if an item of information disputed by a consumer is found to be inaccurate or incomplete or cannot be verified after any reinvestigation under paragraph (1), for purpose of reporting to a consumer reporting agency only, as appropriate, based on the results of the reinvestigation promptly -

      i. modify that item of information;

      ii. delete that item of information; or

      iii. permanently block the reporting of that item of information

2. Deadline. A person shall complete all investigations, reviews, and reports required under paragraph (1) regarding information provided by the person to a consumer reporting agency, before the expiration

of the period under section 611(a)(1) [15 USC §1681i(a)(1)] within which the consumer reporting agency is required to complete actions required by that section regarding that information.

There is one major exception to the rule that you need to dispute an item with the credit bureau. If the furnisher of information is a "debt collector," the provision of inaccurate information to a credit bureau may violate the Fair Debt Collection Practices Act (FDCPA); 15 U.S.C. §1692e(8) provides that it is a violation of the FDCPA to communicate or threaten to communicate credit information that is known to be or should be known to be false, including the failure to communicate that a disputed debt is disputed.

Collection agencies often violate this section by failing to report the fact that a debt is disputed to the credit bureaus after receiving a dispute from a consumer. This entitles the consumer to sue for statutory damages under the FDCPA but not the FCRA. It is not necessary to prove actual damages in such a case.

Debt collectors include collection agencies, collection lawyers, and (in most jurisdictions) companies that purchase delinquent debts.

NOTE

Other common FCRA violations involve obtaining reports without a permissible purpose and failing to comply with the procedures for using consumer reports (including background checks and other nonfinancial reports) by employers and landlords. If you have been denied employment or a rental because of a "consumer report," consult an attorney.

Note that although the written permission of the subject of the report constitutes a "permissible purpose," permission is not required if a permissible purpose otherwise exists, such as a request for credit. There is a common misconception that a creditor cannot obtain a credit report without the consumer's permission, but that is not correct.

Under the FCRA, a successful lawsuit requires either (a) negligence plus injury that was caused by the inaccuracy or (b) a willful violation. If a dispute is required, only damages that occurred after the consumer sent the dispute letter are recoverable.

The statute of limitations under the FCRA is two years from discovery or five years from the violation, whichever is shorter. The statute of limitations under the FDCPA is one year.

The Scope and Nature of Identity-Theft Crime

According to statistics compiled by the Federal Trade Commission (FTC), identity theft tops the list of consumer complaints. The FTC received 332,646 reports of identity theft in 2015. This may represent a fraction of the actual cases. The FTC has estimated that over 27 million Americans have been victimized by this crime.

The consequences of identity theft for the victim include loss of money taken from bank accounts, damage to or destruction of credit, difficulty opening bank accounts and maintaining banking relationships, harassment by debt collectors for debts that are not the creditor's, Internal Revenue Service (IRS) problems, and attribution to the creditor of criminal offenses that were committed by others.

Who Is the Biggest Threat to Stealing Your Identity?

Various methods are used by thieves to steal your identity, such as the following:

- Dumpster diving (going through your personal and public trash, searching for bills or other paperwork containing information that can be used to open accounts in your name);
- Stealing mail, including bank and credit card statements, preapproved offers, new checks, and tax information;
- Skimming (stealing your credit/debit card number, using a special storage device when processing transactions);
- Phishing (posing as companies or financial institutions by sending e-mails or pop-ups for the sole purpose of getting you to reveal your personal identification) and pharming (creating websites similar to those of legitimate businesses, with the same objective);

- Changing your address (to divert your billing statements to another address by completing a "change of address form");
- Stealing wallets or purses; and
- Electronic or physical theft of information from retailers, medical providers, and others that acquired the information legitimately.

Although there has been extensive publicity about electronic means of obtaining information, such as hacking the computer systems of retailers, about 75 percent of all identity theft uses nonelectronic means of obtaining your information, such as stealing wallets, stealing mail, obtaining information from garbage, and dishonest employees obtaining information you provide in transactions.

In addition, a significant proportion of identity theft involves misplaced trust—spouses, other family members, and significant others who obtained access to the victim's information in the course of a relationship and used it or continue to use it without authority to do so. This type of identity theft is particularly troublesome because creditors, credit bureaus, and others often refuse to treat such a case as identity theft unless you are willing to prosecute the perpetrator, reasoning that otherwise it would be too easy for you to allow a friend or relative to use your credit and then disclaim responsibility.

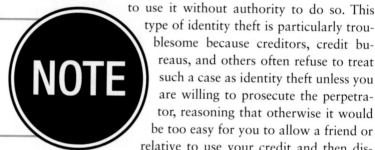

Identity theft may involve using your information or Social Security number to obtain a tax refund, a job, or medical treatment.

If you believe someone has used your Social Security number to obtain a tax refund or job, or you received correspondence from the IRS indicating a problem, contact the IRS immediately and ask for the Identity Theft Specialized Unit. Filing your taxes early helps minimize the use of your Social Security number to file bogus returns in your name.

Common and New Types of Identity Theft

Child identity theft is an increasing problem. Sometimes the perpetrator is a family member with poor credit. Sometimes it is an unrelated third party who obtains the information, often from school records. The scheme is to use a child's Social Security number (existing or new) to apply for governmental benefits, open bank or credit card accounts, or apply for credit. The thief assumes that a child will not apply for credit on his or her own for many years, and the fraud will therefore escape detection.

Telltale signs of this type of identity theft, when perpetrated by unrelated third parties, include the following:

- Denial of government benefits because they are already being provided using the same Social Security number;
- Notification from the IRS indicating financial activity that you don't know anything about;
- Collection communications about transactions you know nothing about.

If you suspect child identity theft, request a credit report from the major bureaus. This is similar to a request made by an adult, but the parent or guardian needs to submit proof of the relationship with the child, such as a birth certificate.

We recommend checking a child's credit reports on the child's sixteenth birthday to see if there are any problems prior to applying for a job, a student loan, or other credit.

Sometimes a parent will use a child's data to open accounts, apply for lines of credit, or apply for benefits. The child does not suspect anything until he or she tries to buy a home or apply for some other loan.

Warning signs include the following:

- Credit card offers come in the child's name or nickname, even though the child doesn't have a bank account.
- The parent or relative struggles financially, then suddenly appears to have money.
- The parent has a history of fraud or misusing others' identities.
- The parent and child live apart, yet the child's name appears on the parent's caller ID system.

If you suspect this has happened, get a copy of your credit report and review it thoroughly to verify that there are items that do not pertain to you. If you confirm parental identity theft, you have two general options for how to handle it: report it to the authorities, or deal with it outside of the system.

If you do not want to be held responsible for the misuse of your credit by a parent, you *must* report the fraud to the authorities *and* be willing to cooperate in the prosecution. If you are not willing to do this, no creditor will treat the account as fraudulent. They will not make it easy for family members to obtain credit and disavow responsibility for it.

Your other option is to work things out with your parent. This means you'll have to sit down with the parent, discuss the issue, and come to an arrangement for repayment. The problem, of course, is that the parent has already demonstrated that he or she is not honest, so the undertaking may not be worth much. (If you do enter into such an undertaking, make certain it is in writing.) In addition, if your credit has been damaged by the parent's failure to repay the credit taken in your name, it will *not* be restored by this course of action. Finally, your failure to repudiate with the creditors the accounts opened in your name may be treated by the law as "ratification," meaning that you may be deemed to have accepted the accounts as if you had authorized them in the first instance. Unless you are certain that you have the financial ability to pay the fraudulent accounts, working things out with your parent is not recommended. If you start along the path of working things out with your parent, you will *not* be able to change your mind later.

Be certain to protect yourself in the future. A credit report monitoring service that alerts you to changes in your credit score, credit reports, and reports to credit bureaus of new addresses and phone numbers associated with you may be necessary to make sure any new debts actually belong to you and that you do not suffer further harm.

Review any statements you get from a medical insurer or provider. See if they reflect any services that you did not obtain.

If a parent's actions are adversely affecting your own financial life, it's probably time to get professional assistance.

Medical identity theft is another problem. An identity thief may use your information to obtain medical services.

Other telltale signs of this type of identity theft include the following:

- Bills or collection communications for medical services you don't recognize;
- Notice from your insurer that you have reached a deductible or benefit limit, which does not seem appropriate; and
- Notices from your insurer that are not consistent with your medical treatment or conditions, such as a denial of coverage for a condition you don't have.

If you believe that this has occurred, follow the procedures set out herein for other cases of identity theft. In addition, ask each of your insurers and medical providers for an accounting of all disclosures of your medical information. You are entitled to one free accounting of disclosures per year. This may indicate other persons you need to contact.

Business ID theft is yet another problem. Not only individuals but small businesses are victims of ID theft. The perpetrators typically file reports with the state that allow them to impersonate companies in good financial standing. Sometimes thieves might change official documentation that lists the address, corporate officers, or registered agents of a business. Using altered documents, they'll get lines of credit in the company's name and siphon off money.

The National Association of Secretaries of State (NASS) recommends the following:

- File your reports and renewals with state filing offices on time.
- Check your business records regularly to make sure information is accurate.
- Even if your business isn't a going concern at the moment, check those records, too. ID thieves often target companies that are no longer in business in the hope their crime will go undetected.

Monitor your bills and accounts for suspicious transactions.

Many state offices responsible for corporate filings offer password protections for online transactions and e-mail notifications when changes are made. Take advantage of these security features.

If you notice unauthorized changes to business records, contact your secretary of state immediately.

Summary

Identity theft is one of the fastest growing crimes in the United States. Most of it is committed using "old-fashioned" means, such as taking advantage of misplaced trust. Pay attention to statements you get from financial institutions, and check your credit regularly.

CHAPTER

23

Safeguarding Your Information from Identity Theft

Where Is Your Information Kept, and How Can You Keep It Safe?

People often do not realize how much information about them is publicly available on the Internet or from public records. Be careful what you post on Facebook and other social media. In particular, be careful about posting such information as your birthday, age, and names of relatives that you may use to answer security questions.

School directories often contain information about children that can be of value to an identity thief, such as dates of birth. The federal Family Educational Rights and Privacy Act (FERPA) gives parents the right to opt out of such publications. This should be done in writing. You may have additional rights under state law.

Keeping Your Information Safe

As noted in the previous chapter, approximately 75 percent of identity theft involves nonelectronic means of obtaining your information.

Lock financial documents and records in a safe place at home.

When discarding mail that contains account numbers and "preapproved" credit offers, shred it instead of just putting it in the trash. Also shred any other financial information you no longer need.

Protect your Social Security number. Do not carry your number, and do not write it on a check. Commit it to memory. Do not give it out unless absolutely necessary.

Never write passwords or personal identification numbers (PINs) on access devices.

Use a locking mailbox, and collect incoming mail promptly. If you have mail pickup from home, don't use it for financial mail; put such mail in an actual postal mailbox.

If no one will be home for several days, have the post office put a hold on your mail deliveries.

Try to use a limited number of passwords for financial accounts or computers that contain personal information that you can commit to memory and cannot be guessed by someone who has information about you or your family.

Keep a list of financial institutions and account numbers in a safe place that can be readily accessed by you and you alone.

Remove and shred labels on prescription bottles before discarding them.

Being Safe Online and on the Telephone

Unless you know whom you are dealing with (i.e., you clearly recognize the caller by voice), never, ever, provide information in response to unsolicited calls or e-mails. "Phishing" scams (inquiries by scammers purporting to be banks, government agencies, or others for the purpose of stealing your personal information) and "pharming" scams (diverting someone seeking a website to one with a similar address operated by the fraudsters) are common and fool a remarkable number of even sophisticated persons.

Do not click on links in e-mails purporting to have pictures or information. This is a common trick used to install malware, viruses, and spyware on computers.

If you receive an e-mail or telephone inquiry purporting to be from a financial institution or medical provider you deal with, do *not* respond directly. Instead, contact the institution at the number/address on the company's statements or its website or that you know belongs to the institution, and ask if the inquiry is in fact from the company.

Beware of communications from persons purporting to offer "free" goods or services but requesting financial or insurance information. This is indicative of either phishing or a telemarketing scam. After all, if something is really free, they don't need such information.

Refrain from using obvious passwords (i.e., date of birth, family names, or the last four digits of your Social Security number). Do not have so many passwords that you need to write them down. Pick one or several totally arbitrary combinations of numbers and letters that you can reliably commit to memory.

Although some have advised that passwords should be changed frequently, this tends to encourage writing down passwords and the use of "weak" passwords that can be remembered easily. A better idea is to have a very "strong" (completely arbitrary) password, memorize it, and don't change it very often.

Be careful what information about yourself you post online. An identity thief can use the information to answer "challenge" questions on accounts. If you can select challenge questions, don't use any for which the answer can be found online.

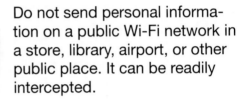

CAUTION Do not send personal information on a public Wi-Fi network in a store, library, airport, or other public place. It can be readily intercepted.

Use antivirus and antispyware software and a firewall, and update them frequently. Hackers use malware to obtain passwords and personal information from computers.

Suspicious Transactions

If you receive inquiries or offers or business opportunities that appear "too good to be true," often by e-mail or fax, they probably are. People are still fooled by the "Nigerian 433" scam (named after a section of that country's penal code), in which they are asked to provide banking information so that they can receive a commission for laundering money for a person located outside the United States.

NOTE Banks are required by law to make funds available within a relatively short period of time. If the check is returned afterward, and the proceeds have been withdrawn, the person depositing the check is liable to the bank.

Do not engage in transactions that involve depositing checks or other instruments for others and giving them part of the proceeds. The transactions are often scams, and the checks are counterfeit or altered. It is difficult to conceive of a legitimate reason why you would be asked to do this. We nevertheless see repeated complaints from persons fooled into doing this, often by persons whom they do not know well enough.

We receive many inquiries from persons who are victims of such scams and complain that the bank did not alert them to the fact that the check they were presenting was counterfeit. Unfortunately, there is generally no obligation on the part of the bank to do this. A person depositing a check

WARNING Avoid scams involving the deposit of checks and payment of proceeds to another. You warrant to the bank in which you deposit a check that it is good. The bank does not warrant anything about the check to you.

warrants to the financial institution that the check is valid and will be paid. The bank accepting the deposit does not warrant anything. The law places the burden on the person receiving and depositing the check to know why he or she is receiving it and whether it is good.

Consider opting out of pre-screened offers for credit and insurance. You can opt out for five years or permanently. Call 888-567-8688, or go to http://www.optoutprescreen.com.

Watch What You Put in the Trash

Shred receipts, credit offers, credit applications, insurance forms, medical statements, checks, bank statements, credit card statements, expired credit and debit cards, and similar documents containing financial information before you throw them away.

Before disposing of a computer or mobile device, remove or overwrite the memory device so as to delete your personal information permanently. Many discarded electronic devices are shipped overseas for parts, creating a significant risk that a crook will try to extract usable information from memory devices.

Destroy labels on prescription containers before you throw them out. Medical identity theft is an increasing problem, and the information on prescription labels (names of medical providers and drugs you take, which often indicates your medical conditions) can facilitate it.

Use Discretion in Private Places

Keep information such as your Social Security number, date of birth, personal identifying numbers, passwords, banking information, and account information secure from outside employees such as housekeepers or cleaning persons working in your home. If possible, keep it under lock and key, or don't write it down at all. Again, 75 percent of identity theft involves physical misappropriation of financial information, often by persons you trust.

Monitor Your Bank and Credit Card Statements and Credit Reports

Review your bank statements, credit card statements, and other financial statements carefully, periodically, and routinely. Look for unexpected activities or items that are not yours or that you don't recognize. Monitor when statements arrive. If you do not get a statement when you expect it to arrive, check—diversion of statements is one sign of identity theft.

If you notice items on your statement that you didn't make or cannot recognize, contact your financial institution immediately, following up in writing. In the case of a credit card or debit card account, label the letter a "billing error notice." Make sure you put your name, address, and account number on the correspondence. If it appears that the transaction is the result of identity theft, as opposed to an accounting error by the financial institution (these do happen), file a formal complaint with your local police department, and provide any necessary information they request.

Review bank statements promptly, and notify the bank of unauthorized or erroneous transactions immediately. If you do not get a bank statement when you expect one, contact the bank immediately as well. Otherwise, you may be liable for the transactions.

Often, banks are entitled by contract or statute to prompt notice—thirty or sixty days after a statement is sent—of any unauthorized or erroneous transactions. Courts generally enforce such requirements. We receive many complaints from people about unauthorized debits that occurred over a period of a year or more, and there is often nothing that can be done.

If you fail to provide notice to the institution of an unauthorized transaction, not only the particular transaction but subsequent transactions of the same nature may be considered authorized or to be the result of your negligence—and thus your responsibility. It is therefore critical that you look at financial statements immediately upon receipt and notify the financial institution of anything you do not recognize. If you give oral notice, follow it up in writing.

If you do not get a statement when you should, contact the institution and arrange to get one. In fact, redirection of statements is one means of carrying out identity-theft crimes.

Note that you do not have to be certain that a transaction is unauthorized to question it—if you do not recognize a transaction, it is perfectly proper to write and state that you cannot identify the transaction and request a copy of the documentation for it so that you can see if it was proper. Doing so protects your rights as long as you inform the bank whether or not the transaction is yours upon receipt of any documentation. If the bank is not able to provide documentation, it has to reverse the transaction.

People who do not review statements and are victimized by identity theft incur an average loss of nearly $20,000. When people who promptly review their statements are victimized, the average loss is less than $6,000. Furthermore, because limitations on liability are conditioned on prompt notice, the people with the $20,000 losses may bear some or all of it themselves.

Summary

In order to minimize the risk that you will become a victim of identity theft, it is important that you safeguard your information and avoid questionable transactions.

CHAPTER

24

What to Do If You Are a Victim of Identity Theft

Recognizing That Your Identity Has Been Stolen

Telltale signs of identity theft include the following:

- Bills/collection contacts/financial institution statements concerning transactions you know nothing about
- Inquiries on your credit reports from businesses that you do not recognize or have not done business with
- Information/transactions on your credit report that do not belong to you (this can also be a "mixed-file" problem)
- Changes in your credit score that are not consistent with your own credit activity
- Notices from businesses that your information has been compromised by a data breach
- Failure to receive bills/statements you expect to receive (because they have been rerouted by the identity thief)
- Your checks being refused acceptance

Repairing Damage to Your Credit Report—Reports You Must File

Identity-theft victims must go through a lengthy and sometimes frustrating process to correct the harm. It is important to act promptly, document all actions taken, and insist that creditors and credit bureaus comply with their legal obligations.

If you suspect that accounts were opened through identity theft, call the creditors involved. Ask for the fraud department. Explain that someone stole your identity. Insist that they close or freeze the accounts, so no one can add new charges unless you agree. Change all logins, passwords, and personal identification numbers (PINs) for your accounts. Send a letter to each creditor confirming your report. Keep a copy.

Victims of identity theft need to promptly file an identity-theft police report and fill out a Federal Trade Commission (FTC) identity-theft affidavit (the form is on the FTC website at http://www.consumer.ftc.gov/articles/pdf-0094-identity-theft-affidavit.pdf) and save a copy. Submit the report and affidavit to each credit bureau, specifying the information on the report that is not yours. Also include your name, address, and Social Security number. If you submit a police report and affidavit, the credit bureaus are required to block the information and "tradelines" from appearing on your report. Also submit a copy to the FTC.

The contact information of the major credit bureaus for this purpose are as follows as of June 2015:

Equifax.com
P.O. Box 105069
Atlanta, GA 30348-5069
1-800-525-6285
Fax 770-375-2821

Experian.com
P.O. Box 2104
Allen, TX 75013
1-888-397-3742

TransUnion.com
Fraud Victim Assistance Department
P.O. Box 6790
Fullerton, CA 92634
1-800-680-7289
Fax 714-447-6034

These numbers and addresses change from time to time, so check before use.

Once the information is blocked, it won't show up on your credit report, and companies can't try to collect the debt from you.

The complaint form is not available on mobile devices, but you can call 1-877-438-4338 to make your report.

Print and save your FTC identity-theft affidavit immediately. Once you leave the page, you won't be able to get your affidavit.

Victims should also contact the credit bureaus and ask them to put an extended fraud alert or a security freeze on their credit files to prevent further damage. This can be done orally with written confirmation.

If you contact one of the three credit bureaus, that company is required to tell the other two. However, we recommend contacting all three.

A security freeze prevents all access to your credit report. It does not prevent misuse of existing accounts by an identity thief. If you want to apply for credit yourself, you must ask the credit bureau(s) to lift the freeze, permanently or temporarily.

A fraud alert allows access to your credit report but advises creditors to contact you by telephone before extending credit. (This is a request; contact is not mandatory, but most creditors comply.) We suggest a fraud alert so that you can continue obtaining credit.

There is no charge for a fraud alert; there may be a charge for a freeze, depending on state law.

A fraud alert entitles you to two free credit reports within two months and requires that you be removed from marketing lists based on prescreening of credit reports for five years. The alert stays in place for seven years.

Under the Fair Credit Reporting Act (FCRA), identity-theft victims have the right to request from the credit grantor the credit application and other documents relating to the account opened by the ID thief. We strongly recommend doing this because the documents (e.g., signatures and addresses on an application) may help victims prove that they did not open the account themselves. Make the requests in writing and keep a copy. Some creditors, mainly smaller ones, may not understand that they have to provide this information, so insist that they do so.

Closing Accounts

Identity-theft victims should promptly contact any company that has issued credit in their name, inform them of the fraud, and demand that they immediately close the account. If you do this orally, send written confirmation afterward, and ask for written acknowledgment that the account has been closed, that you are not being held responsible for it, and that it is being removed from your credit report. Most large credit grantors have a fraud department; ask for that department.

Write down whom you contacted and when. Keep copies of all correspondence.

As soon as possible, send the creditor a copy of your police report and FTC ID theft affidavit. The company may request these items. However, do not delay providing notification until these documents are available.

If you receive collection letters on an account that is not yours, send a similar letter and provide the same documentation. Try to do so within thirty days of receipt of the initial collection letter to preserve your rights under the Fair Debt Collection Practices Act (FDCPA), where applicable.

Removing Unauthorized Charges from Accounts

If the problem is that the identity thief placed bogus charges on accounts that you did open, the procedure is similar. Call the fraud department of each business. Explain that someone stole your identity. Tell them which charges are fraudulent— be very careful to specify which charges are clearly unauthorized and which you have questions about. Send a confirming letter.

Ask the business to remove the bogus charges. Ask the business to send you a letter confirming the fraudulent charges were removed, that you are not being held liable for them, and that credit reporting will not include the fraudulent charges.

Write down whom you contacted and when. Keep copies of all correspondence.

The business may require you to send it a copy of your identity theft report or complete a special dispute form. Provide this information.

Other Steps That You May Need to Take

Tax-Related Identity Theft

If you receive a notice from the Internal Revenue Service (IRS) indicating that a tax return has been filed using your Social Security number or tax ID number, call the IRS right away.

Complete IRS Form 14039, Identity Theft Affidavit. Mail or fax the form according to the instructions. Include proof of your identity, such as a copy of your Social Security card, driver's license, or passport.

Did the notice say you were paid by an employer you don't know? Send a letter to the employer explaining that someone stole your identity and that you don't work for the employer.

File your tax return, and pay any taxes you owe. You might have to mail paper tax returns.

Write down whom you contacted and when. Keep copies of any letters you send.

If these steps don't resolve your situation, contact the IRS's Identity Protection Unit at 1-800-908-4490.

Opening New Accounts

Victims of ID theft should request credit card companies and banks to issue new account numbers. Make sure that they are notified that the prior information was or may have been compromised and that they should not automatically transfer activity on the old account to the new one. Confirm such instructions in writing.

Change all passwords and PINs used prior to the incident, on all accounts.

Summary

Prompt action can mitigate or avoid financial loss from identity theft. File a police report, fill out the FTC identity-theft affidavit, and notify the creditors and credit bureaus.

Epilogue

As attorneys who represent consumers in consumer credit and collection cases, we see many people who get into trouble in consumer credit transactions. We have attempted to provide information to help you stay out of trouble or deal with it if a problem arises.

It is important that you have a basic understanding of your rights and obligations with respect to obtaining credit and protecting your credit record.

The law requires that you be provided with advance information regarding terms of proposed credit transactions. However, many people get into disadvantageous or unaffordable credit transactions because they do not understand or do not use the information furnished.

The law also gives you substantial rights if something goes wrong with a credit transaction. If you do not get what you bargained for, you have rights. If you are unable to repay, you also have rights. If a problem arises with respect to your credit report or credit score, you have rights.

Most of the laws that regulate consumer credit provide for statutory damages and an award of attorney's fees against the business. You should not hesitate to consult an attorney if you have a problem.

Index

A

Access devices, 39
Actual damages, 55
Adjustable-rate mortgages, 13
Administrative wage garnishment, 23, 24, 43
Adverse action, 87
  notice, 1, 93
African American consumers, 19
Amortization period, 30
Amounts owed, 84
Annual percentage rates (APRs), 6, 9, 10, 13, 20, 21, 32, 85, 95
Antispyware software, 111
Antivirus, 111
Arbitration clauses, 33
Asset accounts, 39
Attorneys, collection, 61–62
Authorized user, of credit card, 28, 29, 64
Auto creditors, 69
Auto financing, recurrent problem with, 21
Auto title loans, 45
Automated dialing equipment, use of, 52
Automated telephone-dialing equipment, 72
Automated teller machines (ATMs), 39
Automatic payments, 85
Automobile, 48
  deficiencies, 69–70

B

Bad-check statutes, 48, 64
Bad debts, buyer of, 48
Bail bonds, 10
Balance billed, 67
Balance, credit card, 9
  transferring, 10, 11, 12
Bank statements
  monitoring, 112–113
  review, 40
Bankruptcy, 24, 96
Billing cycles, 29
Billing errors, 27–28
  notice, 112
Borrowers, 17–18, 44
Brokers, 13
  mortgage, 14–15
Business ID theft, 106
Business model, 61

C

Car dealers, 3, 6
Car loan
  negotiating, 19–21
  servicing, 21
Card issuer, 97
Cardholder agreements, disclosure of, 33

Cash advances, 10, 29, 31
Casino gaming chips, 10
Cell phone calls, special rules regulating, 52–53
Certegy, 82
Chargemaster, 68
Charges, 14
Chase bank, 63
Checks, dishonored, 48, 64
ChexSystems, 82
Child identity theft, 104–105
Closed-end credit
    accounts, 86
    transactions, 6–7
Collecting Consumer Debts: The Challenges of
        Change: A Federal Trade Commission
        Workshop Report, 57
Collection accounts, paying off, 86–87
Collection agencies, 47, 102
Collection attorneys, 61–62
Collection calls, dealing with, 71–74
Collection claims, defenses to, 63–70
    automobile deficiencies, 69–70
    credit card accounts
        bogus charges on, 63
        capacity of parties to, 64
    defective goods and services, 70
    health-care debts, 67–69
    liability
        of children for parent's debts, 66
        of parents and spouses, 65–66
    nursing home debts, 66
    promises to answer for debt of another, 65
    statutes of limitations, 64–65
Collection industry, 57–60
Collection lawsuit, defendant in, 61–62
Collection lawsuits, filed, 54
Collection lawyers, 47
Communication
    by answering machines, 51
    with debtor, 51–52
    by postcard, 51
    by voicemail system, 51
Community property states, 65
Computer systems, hacking, 104
Condominium and homeowners' association
        assessments, 48
Consent, 53
Consent agreement, 91
Consent foreclosures, 87
Consent order, 21
Consolidation loan, 44
Consumer, 48, 59–60, 68–69, 71, 73
    written notice to, 49–50

Consumer-arranged financing, 20
Consumer credit counseling services, 73
Consumer Credit Protection Act, 1
Consumer Financial Protection Bureau (CFPB), 11,
        15, 19, 24, 33, 35, 36, 37, 39, 43, 44, 59, 60,
        63, 65, 83, 94
Consumer Leasing Act, 1
Consumer protection laws, 69
Consumer report, 81, 82, 102
Consumer reporting agencies, 81–82, 87, 90,
        92–93, 99, 100
Consumers, 2, 6, 11, 17, 19, 36, 40, 41
    credit limit for, 31
    credit report, 21
    debt, collection of, 47
    loan agreement, 21
    prepaid, 35
    under water, 6, 21
Contractual relationship, 48
Cooling-off period, 7
Credit
    account
        closed-end, 86
        closing, 84
        open-end, 86
    application, to financial institution, 95
    applications, information on, 3
    applying for
        rights in, 1–2
        warnings about, 2–3
    closed-end, 6–7
    denial of, 87
    documentation, 2
    at higher rate, 46
    history, 83–84
        amounts owed, 84
    inquiries on credit score, 85
    open-end, 7–8
    permissible purpose for, 102
    problems, 75
    reports
        cleaning up errors on, 87–88
        rights with respect to, 81–94
        tradelines, 89
        types of information on, 88–92
        who can get, 92
    score, 76
    and spending, 75–79
    terms of, 5–8, 20
    tips for responsible use of, 75–79
    total cost of, understanding, 5–8
    turned down for, 46
Credit-based insurance score, 83

Credit billing, 27–28
Credit bureaus, 1, 2, 12, 81, 82, 89, 90, 99, 101–102, 104, 115–116
  algorithms, 88
  rejects disputes, 91
Credit card
  account, 95–96
    bogus charges on, 63
    capacity of parties to, 64
  advertisements, 9–10
  authorized user, 28, 29
  balance, carrying, 9
  cash advances for, 10
  close or cancel, 30
  companies, 30–33, 83
  debts, 48
  fees for maintenance of, 32
  financing, 11
  grace period, 10
  holders, 28
  interest rates, 8, 11
  issuers, 28, 29, 31, 32, 36–37, 63, 70
  limit, 9
  minors and students, special protections for, 32
  offers, 10
    complaints for, 11
  plan to use, 9
  rates, 10, 30
  rights, 27–33
    arbitration clauses, 33
    credit billing, 27–28
    defective goods and other claims and defenses, 29
    disclosure of terms of cardholder agreements and free credit reports, 33
    rights of consumers in credit card transactions, 30–33
    unauthorized use, 28–29, 40
  secured, 96–97
  selecting, 9
  shopping for, 9–12
  spending limit, 12
  statements, challenging, 27–28
  statements, monitoring, 64, 112–113
  transactions, rights of consumers in, 30–33
  unauthorized use, 28–29, 40
Credit Card Accountability Responsibility and Disclosure (CARD) Act, 5, 10, 30, 36
Credit grantors, 85, 117
Credit insurance, 14
Credit obligation, 21
Credit repair organizations, 27, 91

Credit Repair Organizations Act, 1
Credit report, 45
  fees, 14
  firms, 91
  inquiries on, 115
  monitoring service, 105, 112–113
  problem, hiring lawyer to deal with, 99–102
  repairing damage to, 115–117
  reports, 59
Credit score, 9, 12
  calculation of, 83
  changes in, 115
  credit inquiries on, effect of, 85
  do not consider, 84
  hard inquiries, 85
  improving, 85–86, 95–97
  soft inquiries, 85
Credit transaction, 1
Credit unions, 20, 24
Creditor, 1, 7, 15, 28, 29, 41, 44, 48, 52, 65, 69, 71, 73, 77, 81–82, 96, 102, 104, 115–116, 117
Criminal case, example of, 59

D
Dealers, 21
  arrange financing, 20
  buy rate to, 19
  mark-ups, 19
Debit cards, 33, 39–41
  unauthorized purchases in, 40
Debt, 57, 64, 65
  of another, promises to answer for, 65
  charging off, 86
  collection, contact lawyer regarding, 73–74
  current owner of, 60
  defined, 48
  health-care, 67–69
  notice of, 49, 71
  nursing home, 66
  prebankruptcy, 96
  reaffirmed, 96
  tagging, 58
  time-barred, 64–65
  verification of, 49–50
Debt burden, 23
Debt buyers, 47, 61–62, 64, 68, 69, 71, 73
  growth of, 59
  versus original creditors, 57–60
Debt collection, 57
  agencies, 89

Debt collectors, 24, 40, 41, 44, 45, 47, 48, 50,
51–52, 57, 58, 61, 102
abuse by, 53
fake, 59, 71–72
identification of, 49
legitimate, 59
make affirmative disclosures to debtors, 49
Debtors
communication with, 51–52
delinquent, 53
false, misleading, and unfair acts and practices,
53–54
Defective Goods and Services, 70
Defense, 64
Degree of evidence, 50
Delinquent obligations, 82
Denial of coverage, 106
Department of Education, 43
Department of Housing and Urban Development, 15
Department of Justice (DOJ), 19
Department of Veterans Affairs, 13
Department store credit cards, 29
Disclosure requirements, 7
Discover Bank, 63
Discover Financial Services, 24
Discrimination, risks of, 19
Dispute-resolution process, improving, 91
Disputed accuracy, procedure in case of, 99–100
Disputed information, reinvestigations of, 99–101
Dodd–Frank Wall Street Reform and Consumer
Protection Act (Dodd–Frank Act), 5, 7, 10
Down payment, 14
Draconian collection methods, 23, 43
Dumpster diving, 103

E
Early Warning, 82
Educational credit scores, 83
Electronic devices, discarded, 112
Electronic fund transactions, 39–41
Electronic fund transfer, 39–40
recurring or preauthorized, 41
Electronic Fund Transfer Act (EFTA), 32, 35, 39–40, 41
Emergency Economic Stabilization Act of 2008, 5
Employment background checks, 93–94
Equal Credit Opportunity Act (ECOA), 1, 46, 65, 81
Equifax, 82
Error-resolution
procedures, 41
rights, 35
Escrow account, 14
Experian, 82
Exportation, of interest rates, 7
Express informed consent, 21

Extraordinary collection actions, 69

F
Fair Credit Billing provisions, of TILA, 27, 29
Fair Credit Reporting Act (FCRA), 1, 81–82, 90,
94, 99, 102, 117
Fair Debt Collection Practices Act (FDCPA), 1, 44,
45, 47, 48, 50, 59, 64, 72, 89, 102, 117
abuse and harassment, 53
affirmative disclosures to debtors, 49
collection lawsuits, filed, 54
communication with debtor, 51–52
damages, 55
false, misleading, and unfair acts and practices,
53–54
purpose of, 48
statute of limitations, 102
Fair Isaac Corporation (FICO), 9, 83, 86, 95–96
score, 13, 83, 84, 85, 87
Fake debt collectors, 59
Federal Communications Commission (FCC), 53, 72–73
Federal consumer protection laws, 84
Federal Family Educational Rights and Privacy Act
(FERPA), 109
Federal Housing Administration (FHA), 13
Federal Patient Protection and Affordable Care Act
(Obamacare), 69
Federal Reserve Board, 65
Federal Student Aid Ombudsman Group at the
Department of Education, 44
Federal student loans, 23–25, 43–44
Federal Trade Commission (FTC), 20, 21, 50,
55, 66, 78, 103
identity-theft affidavit, 116, 117
regulation, 69
reports, 57, 60
press release by, 58
Federal Truth in Lending Act (TILA), 5, 6
Fee-harvester credit cards, 9, 32
Fee notices on ATMs, 41
Fees, 10, 11, 14, 17, 31, 32
not refundable, 13
FICO, *See* Fair Isaac Corporation
Filial responsibility statutes, 66
Finance charges, 6, 21, 31, 32, 69
Finance company, 20
Financial assistance, 69
Financial institutions, 3, 35–36, 39–40, 41,
112–113
insured, 96
regulator, 45
Firewall, 111
Fixed-rate loans, 13
Flood-hazard area, 14

Flood insurance, 14
Forbearance agreements, 44
Foreclosure alternatives, 87
Foreclosure lawyers, 47
Foreign currency, purchase of, 10
Fraud alert, 117
Fraud department, 117
Fraudulent charges, 35–36, 117–118
Free Application for Federal Student Aid
    (FAFSA), 25
Free credit reports, disclosure of, 33
Furnishers of information, duties of, 101–102

G
Gap protection, 21
Gasoline company credit cards, 29
General-purpose reloadable cards, 35
Generic credit scores, 83
GI Bill benefits, 23
Gift cards, 35
Goods
    defects in, 69
    and services, defective, 70
Grace period, 31–32
    for credit card, 10

H
Hackers, 111
Harassment, 53
Health-care debts, 67–69
    collection suits for, 67
Helping Families Save Their Homes Act of 2009, 5
High-interest loans, 45
Hispanic consumers, 19
Home mortgage, 12
    loan, negotiating, 13–16
Home Ownership and Equity Protection Act (HOEPA)
    of 1994, 5, 7
Hospital bills, 69
    errors in, 67–68

I
Identity Protection Unit, 118
Identity theft, 88
    being safe online and on telephone, 110–111
    common and new types of, 104–106
    methods used by thieves to steal, 103–104
    police report, 116
    recognizing, 115
    safeguarding information from, 109–113
    scope and nature of, 103–106
    suspicious transactions, 111–112
    tax-related, 118
    telltale signs of, 104, 106, 115

    use discretion in private places, 112
    victims of, 115–118
        closing accounts, 117
        opening new accounts, 118
        other steps that need to take, 118
        removing unauthorized charges from accounts,
            117–118
    watch what you put in trash, 112
Identity Theft Affidavit, 50, 116, 118
Identity Theft Specialized Unit, 104
Impound account, 14
Income-based repayment, 43
Individual retirement account (IRA), 75
Information
    being safe online and on telephone,
        110–111
    electronic or physical theft of, 104
    safe, keeping, 109–110
Installment loans, 45, 84
Insurance
    companies, 83
    payments, 14
    policies and plans, 67
    reports prepared on, 92–93
Insurers, 67, 106
Interest rates, 10, 11, 19, 23, 24, 37, 45
Internal Revenue Service (IRS), 104, 118
    Form 1403, Identity Theft Affidavit, 118
    Identity Protection Unit, 118
Internet sites, 18, 27, 33
Internet sources, 91
Introductory rate, 10
Itemized hospital bill, 67

J
Job applicants, reports prepared on, 92–93
Judge-made law, 65

L
Landlords, 93
Late fees, 10, 31, 36
Lawsuit, 51, 59, 64
    collection, defendant in, 61–62
Least sophisticated consumer standard,
    54–55
Lender-paid mortgage insurance (LPMI), 14
Lenders, 3, 13, 14, 15, 20, 21, 24,
    43–44, 45
Liability, 29
    of children for parent's debts, 66
    defense to, 69
    of parents and spouses, 65–66
License to steal, 33
Licensed lenders, 45

Loan
  document, 78
  eligible for, 13
  fixed-rate, 13
  high-interest, 45
  other types of, 45–46
  payments of, 13
  processing fees, 14
  rehabilitation, 44
  servicing, 17
  variable-rate, 13
Long form disclosure, 36
Lottery tickets, purchase of, 10

M
Mail
  discarding, 109
  stealing, 103
Mailbox, locking, 110
Margins, 13
Material disclosures, 15
Meaningful disclosure, 49
Medicaid and Medicare statutes, 67
Medicaid payments, 66
Medical bill, 67
Medical chart, 67
Medical collection items, 92
Medical debts, 68, 83, 91–92
Medical identity theft, 106, 112
Medical providers, 106
Medical record, items improperly
    billed in, 67–68
Medicare payments, 66
Military tuition assistance, 23
Minimum Payment Warning, 7
Mixed-file problem, 88
Money
  borrowing, rights for, 1–3
  orders, 10
Mortgage
  borrowers, 15
    substantive protections for, 7
  broker, 3, 14–15
  company, 18
  debts, 48
  insurance, 14
  lenders, 12
  loans, 17
  loans, 7, 13, 14
  servicers, 17–18, 21, 47
Mortgage Disclosure Improvement Act
    of 2008, 5
Motor Vehicle Retail Installment Sales
    Act, 50

N
National Association of Secretaries of State
    (NASS), 106
National credit bureaus, 82, 87
National loan vocabulary, 5
Nigerian 433 scam, 111
Non-community-property states, 65
Noncompliance, 7, 62, 69, 78
Notice of error, to mortgage company, 17
Notwithstanding contract, 66
Nursing home debts, 66

O
Open-end credit, 7–8
  accounts, 86
Original creditors, 60, 61–62
  versus debt buyers, 57–60
Origination fees, 24
Outstanding obligation, 21
Over-the-limit transactions, 31
Overdraft protection, 41, 45–46

P
Parental identity theft, 105
Patients, 67
Payback arrangement, negotiating, 73
Payday loans, 45
  debt trap, 75
Payment, 7, 24, 31, 37, 68, 76
  plan, 62
Payoff balances, 7
Payroll cards, 35
Penalties, 31
Penalty rate, 10
Perkins loans, 23
Permissible purposes, for credit, 2
Permitted information, 51
Person furnishing information, 99
Person-to-person money transfers, 10
Person using information, 99
Personal liability, 65
Petition for Expedited Declaratory Ruling and
    Exemption, 73
Pharming, 103
  scams, 110
Phishing, 103
  scams, 110
PLUS loans, 23
PLUS Score, 83
Potential liability, 39
Prepaid cards, 35–37
Prepaid companies, 36–37
Prepaid issuers, 36
Prepayment penalty, 14

Prerecorded messages, 52
Principal residence, 15
Private arbitrators, 33
Private lenders, 24
Private student loans, 23–25
Private vocational schools, 23
Professional bill reviewers, 68
Professional repossessors, 48
Promotional rates, 11, 32
Property insurance, 14
Public companies, 96
Public court records, misreporting
        information from, 89

Q
Qualified written request, to mortgage company, 17

R
Ratification, 105
Re-aging, 89
Real Estate Settlement Procedures Act, 13, 17, 50
Refinancing, 24
Regulation B, 65
Rehabilitation programs, 44
Remittance transfers, 41
Repairing a Broken System: Protecting Consumers
        in Debt Collection Litigation and
        Arbitration, 57
Reserve account, 14
Residential apartment, rent for, 48
Retail Installment Sales Act, 50
Reverse competition by economists, 17
Reward cards, 9
Rights, as debtor, 47–55
    abuse and harassment, 53
    collection lawsuits, filed, 54
    damages, 55
    debtor, communication with, 51–52
    debts, verification of, 49–50
    false, misleading, and unfair acts and practices,
        53–54
    special rules regulating cell phone calls, 52–53
    third-party contacts, 50–51
    unsophisticated or least sophisticated consumer
        standard, 54–55
Rights of consumers in credit card transactions, 30–33
Robocalls, 53
Rules and Regulations Implementing the Telephone
        Consumer Protection Act of 1991, 73

S
Safety and soundness standards, 3
Scammers, 59–60
School directories, 109

Securities and Exchange Commission, 96
Servicers, mortgage, 17–18
Servicing income, 17
Settlement agreement, 73
Short form disclosure, 36
Side agreement, signed, 79
Skimming, 103
Social Security number, 85, 88–89, 95, 104, 118
Social Security payments, 24, 43
Special Assistance Unit, 44
Stafford loans, 23
State attorney general, 45
State installment sales, 69
Statement of Policy Regarding Communications in
        Connection with the Collection of Decedents'
        Debts, 66
Statute of limitations, 23, 24, 49, 62, 64–65, 70, 102
Statutes of frauds, 65, 78, 79
Statutory damages, 55
    substantial, 45
Statutory violation, 48
Store cards, 11
Structure and Practices of the Debt Buying
        Industry, 57
Student financial aid disbursement cards, 35
Student loan
    obtaining, 23–25
    rights, 43–44
    types of, 23
Subprime credit cards, 9, 10
Subprime transactions, 82
Subsidized direct loans, 23
Substantial default penalties, 43
Substantial statutory damages, 69

T
Tax refunds, 24
    cards, 35
    interception of, 23, 43
Tax-related identity theft, 118
Taxpayer identification number, 85, 95
TeleCheck, 82
Telemarketing scam, 110
Telephone calls, 71
    how to end harassing, 72–73
Telephone Consumer Protection Act (TCPA),
        52–53, 72
Tenants, blacklisting, 93
    and employment screening agencies, list of, 94
    screening reports, 93
Third-party contacts, 50–51
Time-barred debt, 64–65
Tort claims, 48
Trailing interest, 12

Transaction, 48
  for personal use, 6
  suspicious, 111–112
  unauthorized, 113
TransUnion, 82
Traveler's checks, 10
Treasury regulations, 69
Truth in Lending Act (TILA), 1, 15, 27, 35, 36, 77
  applicability of, 6–8
  Fair Credit Billing provisions of, 27

U
Unauthorized fund transfer, 39–41
Unauthorized use, of credit card, 28–29, 35–36, 113, 117
Unfair or unconscionable collection methods, 48
Uniform Commercial Code (UCC), 50, 64, 69
  statute of limitations, 70
Universal default, 30, 32
Unlicensed lenders, 45

Unsophisticated consumer standard, 54–55
Usury laws, 7, 45
Utility bills, 96
Utilization rate, 76

V
Validation
  debtor's right to, 49
VantageScore 3, 83, 86
Variable-rate loans, 13
Verification, 50
  debtor's right to, 49
Violation, 64

W
Water and sewer service, 48
Willful violation, 102

Z
Zero balance, 12